INFALLIBILITY AND THE EVIDENCE

INFALLIBILITY AND THE EVIDENCE

by

FRANCIS SIMONS
Bishop of Indore

TEMPLEGATE, PUBLISHERS
Springfield, Illinois 62705

Published in the United States by
Templegate, Publishers,
Springfield, Illinois 62705

Library of Congress Catalog Card No. 68-55376

CONTENTS

FOREWORD

I *Preliminary Remarks*

II *The Evidence: General Observations*

III *Certainty, Infallibility, and the Act of Faith*

IV *Certainty and the Gospels*

V *The Evidence: More General Observations*

VI *The Biblical Evidence for Infallibility*

VII *Papal Power and Infallibility*

VIII *Infallibility and Tradition*

IX *Infallibility and Doctrinal Changes*

POSTSCRIPT

FOREWORD

In Catholic theological literature the case for the Church's infallibility has long since reached its final, conclusive form. Every Catholic student of theology is familiar with the large number of bible texts and theological reasonings on which the doctrine is based. The weight of proof has seemed so overwhelming that the matter has become entirely obvious to him; so much so that the certainty of infallibility has become independent from its biblical foundations and the bible itself is thought unreliable without it. The lean-to appears to support the main building.

The modern "progressive" theologian makes a distinction in his belief in infallibility. He finds more and more reasons for contracting the range of its operation so as to liberate traditional doctrines for renewed discussion, a process similar to the retreat from a position of far-reaching biblical inspiration and inerrancy to the present position which sets definite limits to both. But he also retains faith in the Church's infallibility, as he does in biblical inspiration.

There is even a suspicion that one of the reasons why some theologians retain the doctrine of infallibility is the fact that behind the lean-to and the facade of the main edifice, which now must support each other, they have removed nearly the whole building and its foundations. They practically accept a major postulate of the form-historical school which then, not surprisingly, re-appears as a major conclusion: that since miraculous accounts are unacceptable, we have very few reliable historical data about Christ. The proclamation of the glad tidings – or what is left of it – is gaining some benefit from the doctrine that in proclaiming this the Church is infallible. For a Christian faith which was based on historical evidence for the fact of revelation is substituted a faith of "unconditional trust" that gains stature (and status?) from the weakness of its historical foundations.

Christianity has no future as a revealed religion in an increasingly rational, critical, scientific world if it has no solid historical brief. On the other hand it seems true that the process of dispersing the luminous but obscuring cloud of primitive all-pervading supernaturalism has not gone far enough. Two of its major remains seem to be: belief in a divine inspiration of the bible and belief in ecclesiastical infallibility.

Since the appraisal of the traditional evidence for infallibility has always been considered to lie within the intellectual competence of the ordinary student of theology, who has always been thought capable of assessing the evidence in its favour, this re-examination is now offered to a wider intellectual public. By the very fact that Jesus meant his religion for all the world it must be supposed that the case for its major foundations cannot be of such an abstruse nature that it is only accessible to the critical judgement of a small coterie of specialist scholars.

The thesis here proposed does not only touch the heart of the Catholic system but also the hearts of Catholics. Emotions will be roused which will make it hard to keep the mind open and cool. Besides, the very completeness of the Catholic conviction makes it difficult to take contrary evidence seriously. I was, therefore, tempted to do an unusual thing. As a postscript I wanted to add two instances of the kind of reaction one has to face even from professors of theology. In the end I decided against it. A writer must give himself up to the sense of fair play of his readers. He has no choice. I have benefited much more from those who criticized than from those who approved and I am sincerely grateful to them.

Truth about fundamentals is of fundamental importance. Having come to the conviction that I could prove that the Church's belief in infallibility is mistaken, I felt I had no choice but to publish my case.

One final admission. Though I have read a fair amount of theology and exegesis, I am no expert. Those who are will detect the signs. Still I believe – and on the basis of a briefer, less complete statement experts and others have confirmed me in this – that the substance of my case has been validly demonstrated. If I am proved wrong, I hope I will have done a service to the Church by compelling her to put up a more convincing case.

I

PRELIMINARY REMARKS

Christianity is a historical religion. It claims that God revealed* himself to mankind in Jesus Christ. The evidence advanced by those who saw and heard Christ has been preserved for us in a number of writings bundled together in the books of the New Testament. It is to this evidence that all the Christian churches appeal. In spite of some recurrent extreme criticism, invariably based not on historical but on philosophical or scientistic grounds; i.e., on the prejudice against miracles, the vast majority of scholars and ministers of the Christian churches hold fast, on what seems historically irrefutable evidence, that the New Testament witness is authentic and reliable. Here we suppose this to be true, in the way moderate modern scholarship understands these writings.

In addition to the evidence of the New Testament books, the Roman Catholic Church appeals to the living teaching of the Church which can trace her origins back to the time of the Apostles. She claims that Christ instituted a teaching authority, the Apostles and their successors, to which he gave the commission to teach all nations. She claims also that Christ promised to this teaching body or magisterium the

*It would be appropriate to say "reveals", in the present tense, since Christ's revelation is meant for all times and reaches out to each of us. As, however, the documents through which his revelation is known were written in the past, for the purpose of this thesis the past-tense is used.

prerogative of infallibility; i.e., such divine assistance that whenever the magisterium teaches some proposition as definitively to be held as belonging to the revealed teaching of Christ, it cannot err.

For the first claim, the institution by Christ of a teaching authority or magisterium, we find a number of his sayings which seem to prove that he did institute it, and in the book of the Acts and in the Epistles we observe it actively engaged in teaching.

Things are different regarding the Catholic claim that Christ promised to this magisterium a prerogative of infallibility. The latest most solemn statement of Catholic doctrine of the Church's teaching office and its infallibility is found in the *Constitution on the Church,* promulgated by the Second Vatican Council, Chapter III, No.25, which is given here in full:

"Among the bishops' principal functions, the preaching of the gospel holds the first place.* For the bishops are heralds of the faith who bring new disciples to Christ; they are authentic teachers, that is, teachers endowed with Christ's authority, who preach to the people committed to them the faith that is to be believed and put into practice; enlightened by the Holy Spirit, they illustrate that faith, bringing to light things both new and old from the treasure-house of revelation (Mt 13:52); they make the faith bear fruit and are on the watch to ward off any error that may threaten their flock (cf. 2 Tim 4: 1-4). The bishops, teaching in communion with the Roman Pontiff are to be looked up to by all as witnesses to divine and catholic truth. The faithful must accept the judgment of their bishop when he speaks in the name of Christ on matters of faith and morals, and adhere to it with religious submission. This religious submission of mind and will is especially due the authentic teaching authority of the Roman Pontiff, even when he is not speaking *ex cathedra;* that is to say: his supreme teaching authority is to be reverently acknowledged, his

*Cf. Council of Trent, Decr. de refor., sess. V. C. 2-n. 9; sess. XXIV, can. 4.

pronouncements sincerely adhered to according to his declared mind and will; the latter can be known either from the character of the documents, or from the frequent repetition of the same doctrine, or from his mode of expressing himself.

"Although the bishops do not enjoy individually the prerogative of infallibility, they nonetheless proclaim Christ's doctrine infallibly whenever, even though dispersed throughout the world, yet remaining in communion among themselves and with the successor of Peter, they authentically teach matters of faith and morals and agree on one position as definitively to be held. This is even more clearly verified when, assembled in an ecumenical council, they are, for the universal Church and in matters of faith and morals, teachers and judges whose definitions demand the assent of faith.

"This infallibility with which our divine Redeemer willed his Church to be endowed when she defines a doctrine of faith or morals, is co-extensive with the deposit of divine revelation which must be religiously guarded and faithfully expounded. The Roman Pontiff, head of the college of bishops, possesses this infallibility in virtue of his office, when, as supreme shepherd and teacher of all the faithful, who confirms his brethen in the faith (cf. Lk 22:32), by a definitive act he proclaims a doctrine that belongs to faith or morals. Any such definition of his is of itself, and not from the consent of the Church, justly styled irreformable, since it is pronounced with the assistance of the Holy Spirit promised to him in Blessed Peter, and therefore needs no approval of others, nor does it allow an appeal to another tribunal. For, in such instances, the Roman Pontiff does not pronounce judgement as a private person; rather, when he thus expounds or defends a doctrine of Catholic faith, he speaks as the supreme teacher of the universal Church, in whom is found in a singular manner the charism of infallibility inherent in the Church. The infallibility promised to the Church is to be found also in the body of bishops when that body exercises the supreme teaching authority conjointly with the successor of Peter. The Church can never fail to give her assent to such definitions because the action of the Holy Spirit sees to the preservation and the progress of Christ's universal flock in the unity of faith.

"When the Roman Pontiff, or the body of bishops with him, define a proposition, their pronouncement is in accord with the revelation itself, to which all must adhere and conform. This revelation, whether written or handed down, is transmitted in its entirety through the legitimate succession of bishops, and above all by the care of the Roman Pontiff himself, and under the guiding light of the Spirit of Truth, is religiously preserved and faithfully expounded in the Church. Its conscientious study and correct formulation, with the help of suitable means, are promoted with due zeal and diligence by the Roman Pontiff and the bishops, as befits their office and the importance of the matter. But they do not accept any new public revelation as pertaining to the deposit of faith."

There are three ways in which the teaching office is exercised infallibly:

by the bishops dispersed throughout the world (the ordinary infallible magisterium);

by the same bishops assembled in an ecumenical council; and

by the Roman Pontiff alone.

The second and third are extraordinary ways of exercising the infallible magisterium and cover a smaller field of doctrinal propositions than the first. Infallibility is, however, not restricted to the magisterium, but is shared by the whole Church: "Because they are anointed by the Holy One (cf.1 Jn.2, 20.27), the faithful as a body cannot err in their belief. They manifest this special prerogative of theirs by means of a supernatural sense of faith that belongs to the people as a whole, when 'from the bishops down to the last believer', they show universal agreement in matters of faith and morals" (Vatican II, *Constitution on the Church,* Ch. II, No. 12).

The deposit of divine revelation, which is the object of infallible teaching, is taught to include not only what Christ revealed during his stay on earth, but also what was revealed to the Apostles after Christ's ascension into heaven. Only with the death of the last Apostle did the revelation come to an end. However, infallibility is claimed to extend also to truths which are so intimately connected with the revealed truth that they either follow from it necessarily, or that their denial would logically lead to its denial or deprive the Church of the effective means to protect it, including such facts as the legitimacy of a pope or the convocation of an ecumenical council, or the meaning of texts. To these have to be added other decisions needed to guarantee the indispensable role of the Church for the sanctification of men, including the canonization of saints.

It is admitted by Catholic theologians that not all infallible doctrines can be traced back with certainty to Christ and the Apostles. Ordinarily an argument from tradition would be understood as historical evidence that a doctrine or practice can be traced back, as generally and firmly held by the Church, in uninterrupted sequence to the apostolic age. This is not its meaning in Catholic theology, though in this paper, in the course of argument, it will sometimes have this meaning. As a theological criterion an argument from tradition is considered valid if it can be proved that for some time a doctrine has been generally held as certainly revealed. In such a case it is of course *supposed* – which is essential to the system – that the doctrine does in fact go back to the Apostles or Christ. It means that the claim is made that the living magisterium of the Church is a source of certainty of knowledge about the revelation, in addition to the authentic written sources. Whenever the Church is entirely convinced that a religious or moral proposition is part of the revealed deposit, she teaches it with the assurance that under the guidance of the Spirit she does so infallibly, even though there is no convincing evidence that the proposition belongs to the original revelation or is inseparably connected with it.

Theologians have a hard time to explain *how* the Church can be certain of propositions which cannot be proved to be part of the original revelation. Elaborate and ingenious constructions have not been able to clear up the mystery. The final appeal is, therefore, to the assistance of the Holy Spirit promised by Christ.

Faced with doctrinal changes and new doubts, some theologians have begun greatly to restrict what was traditionally considered to fall within the range of the Church's infallible teaching authority; they deny, for example, that natural moral law, unless also revealed, falls within its scope, or they assert that generally accepted doctrines, which are not clearly contained in the bible nor infallibly defined, are mere ecclesiastical instead of apostolic traditions. This makes it possible practically to eliminate the ordinary infallible magisterium and to discount all traditional doctrines as fallible that do not meet either of the conditions mentioned. In the case of doctrines not clearly contained in the bible, infallible definitions would be the only (a *post factum)* means to distinguish apostolic from ecclesiastical traditions. Even such definitions, being inadequate expressions of revealed realities, are subject to reinterpretation. This latter consideration has opened the way to a great deal of new theological speculation about the historically variable expressions and diverse personal perceptions of truth. If Christianity had first successfully penetrated Hindu instead of Greek culture, the understanding and expression of it would have taken a very different form. These are momentous theological developments comparable in importance with the evolution from biblical literalism to modern principles of bible interpretation.

This paper does not enter into these speculations. It considers the traditional positions and arguments which are still commonly accepted and generally current in theological literature of a few years ago, (for example, in the voluminous *Katholische Dogmatik* of Michael Schmaus, Band III, 1, 1958), and which also survive in the acceptance of the main position on infallibility by the newer theologians. These have begun to whittle down, on reasonable grounds, the wide range of traditional infallibility, but with Vatican II they continue to retain its substantial structure. A scrutiny of the traditional arguments seems to prove that that very structure has to be abandoned.

II

THE EVIDENCE: GENERAL OBSERVATIONS

All major churches believe that God revealed himself to man in Christ. All are willing to accept what Christ revealed. But the question is: how do we know the contents of his revelation? There must be a channel of certain knowledge. For the churches of the Reformation the only channel is the bible. For the Catholic Church the main channel, even the ultimately only reliable one, is the living magisterium instituted by Christ and still preserved in the Church of Rome. Against a fallible human judgement about the meaning of what the bible says, she appeals to the infallible judgement of the living magisterium. Here lies the main fundamental dissent between Rome and the Reformation.

Because of its intrinsic importance, and because it is the main reason for the continuation of the great western schism, it is worth while to have another look at the evidence. Moreover, within the Catholic Church herself there is an increasing awareness surrounding the doctrine of infallibility. A growing number of doctrines which were considered part of the certain doctrinal partrimony of the Church have proved to be in need of revision, or development, or re-adjustment, in order to meet the new knowledge that has rapidly accumulated. The changes have become so numerous and far-reaching that with many educated Catholics the appeal to ecclesiastical or papal teaching authority has ceased to impress. That very teaching authority is under suspicion. Many are still willing to listen to evidence, but no longer to authoritative decisions as such. Not even when these are conciliar or papal definitions or doctrines that have been generally accepted by the Church. Yet if infallibility can be proved to be part of Christ's revelation, the Church has no choice but to retain it. No "ecumenical" reasons and no spreading doubts among her own members could justify her abandoning it. But if the Scriptures do not support the doctrine, if the texts to which appeal is made suggest or demand another explanation, then it cannot be admitted as valid on the strength of a later tradition. It would be a vicious circle to accept a later tradition of infallibility on the strength of the later tradition of infallibility. The more basic and important a matter is for the Christian faith, the greater the need for valid evidence. God cannot demand that we base our faith on uncertain ground.*

The doctrine of infallibility has of course been integrated with other doctrines (on Revelation, the Church, Scripture, Tradition, the Magisterium) into one connected theological structure in which the parts seem to support each other. Confronted with this the denial of infallibility must appear naturalistic and based on false notions and suppositions on all points on which it conflicts with the supernaturalist system. However, even after having proved** that God revealed himself in Jesus Christ, we are not allowed to introduce more supernatural elements than can be proved. The whole burden of proof lies on him who enlarges the area of the supernatural. On every point the naturalist theory has the prior rights. Only when it is evident that the natural explanation breaks down is it permissible to think of a supernatural one. When, for example, after declaring what is common ground to Christians, that God revealed himself, the

*Objections to this statement arising from the act of faith are dealt with in Chap. III.

**We can distinguish two kinds of proof or evidence. One is of things that can be verified by many or all because they can be repeated or remain accessible. Such is proof based on experiments, or evidence based on a direct perception of things still existing (as the sun or Niagara Falls) or of the correlation of terms (as that two and two make four or that a whole is larger than one of its parts). Even in infallibilist goes on to state, "Revelation essentially calls for and implies an infallible Church" – a key principle in his system, though he does not apply it to ancient Israel – the naturalist will stop him and demand proof. It is not enough for the infallibilist to show that the notions and suppositions of the naturalist come into conflict with his own admirable supernaturalist system. It is not even enough for him to show that his system makes sense, that it is reasonable, that the parts fit well together and seem to support each other. In a house of cards the cards also support one another. The infallibilist has to prove that all the supernatural elements of his system follow with logical necessity from demonstrated premisses. Considering how easily we go wrong when relying on abstract reasoning alone, he has to do more. He has to show that the naturalist position involves itself in contradictions and is unable to account for the relevant biblical and extra-biblical facts. It must be left to the reader to judge which of the two, naturalist or infallibilist, gives the more satisfactory and common-sense explanation of the facts and which has to take recourse to improbable unproved suppositions. Surely, once it has been shown that the texts of the bible, on which the Church has traditionally based her case for infallibility, do not prove it, the infallibilist cannot simply shift his appeal, as if nothing had happened, to a doctrinal structure that was erected on the belief that those texts did prove the case.

this kind of evidence we have to accept most things on faith, for lack of direct personal knowledge. The second kind is of things not or no longer directly accessible. Such is, to others, the existence of an intimate love between two persons, or things or events of the past. In these cases non-participants have to depend on faith. Faith, whether of things present or past, will be more or less compelling according to the number and character of the direct witnesses and other factors. No sane informed person doubts the existence of Niagara Falls or the past upheavals of Reformation and French Revolution. From the nature of the case even some present evidence is accessible only to one or a few and cannot be compellingly demonstrated to others.

In the context of this thesis the words "evidence" and "proof" are nearly always used in the meaning attached to them by historians, not by natural scientists: to indicate the existence of convincing historical evidence for what Jesus has said or done. Sometimes, as in the present text, to express that (with the aid of historically assured miracles) we can be certain that God has testified to the truth of what Jesus taught. What Jesus taught or revealed is a matter of historical evidence; did he, for example, teach (reveal) that he is God? It can never be proved directly. that he is God; but if he taught so and if he showed by miracles that he spoke in the name of God, then his word for it must be accepted (indirect proof). More about the need of proof and the role of miracles later in the text.

Evidence extends also to what logically follows from assured premisses.

Apart from the argument from Scripture, the absolute need of an infallible teaching authority is proved or expressed by theologians in various ways, both when speaking of the role of the Church and that of the successor of Peter. Infallibility is said to be the only effective means by which we can be certain of the divine revelation and its contents; without it we would have no guarantee, no certainty, about the right understanding of the revealed truth. This would become the object of personal opinion, and of endless controversy which could never be resolved. For all practical purposes it would render the revelation impotent, as if it had not taken place. When speaking of the successor of Peter and his infallibility, it is said that if he were not infallible, he could become the victim of error; he would lead his sheep to poisonous pastures, and the gates of hell, or Satan, the father of lies, would prevail over him. His error, the error of the head of the Church, would lead the whole Church into error. It is even concluded that the infallibility of the Church is rooted in papal infallibility; this guarantees and supports that of the Church. It would also be against reason to demand doctrinal obedience to a fallible pope under the threat of excommunication.

Appeal is made also to the experience of the Protestant churches which rejected infallibility and thus fell apart into an increasing number of sects. Without infallibility there is no protection against such divisions and the unity of the Church in faith cannot be preserved.

Admittedly, there is need of permanent certainty about the fact of a divine revelation and its essential contents. If God revealed himself to mankind in Christ, we cannot believe that his revelation will be lost in uncertainty.

But does certainty demand infallibility? Is certainty not possible without it?

In our daily lives we have to make do with ordinary moral certainties even where our life is at stake. Three, four times a day we take food with only a moral certainty that it is not poisoned, and with a similar assurance of safety we travel by train, car, or plane. We do not escape dependence on only moral certainty where religion and morality are concerned. Moral decisions have to be taken without absolute certainty that we do the right thing. Even in the face of death we can have only moral certainty that we are ready to meet our divine Judge. Nor are we perhaps better off if it comes to the very basis of the Christian religion. It finally depends on a historical certainty about the person and mission of Jesus Christ.

There are historical certainties based on such wealth of evidence that they may be called absolute or near-absolute, as that the Reformation and French Revolution took place or about Napoleon and the major facts of his career. We believe that error about such major events is excluded. This conviction is not based on faith in any charism of infallibility we possess, but on the weight of concurring and commonly accepted evidence. Believing Christians have always thought that there is a similar historical evidence for the personality and major facts and teaching of Christ. An absolute or near-absolute historical certainty is the result of a great weight of evidence critically assessed by an educated community; it is achieved and attains permanence only as a common effort.

The difference between ordinary objective certainty and a conviction based on infallibility lies in the ground on which certainty rests. In the case of good ordinary certainty the ground is the available evidence which convinces us that a particular thing happened or is. In the case of infallibility our certainty about a particular event or proposition does not rest on evidence for it (which may or may not exist), but on the belief that those who communicate the event or doctrine have been endowed by God with a prerogative that, under certain conditions, saves them from the possibility of error.

In the case of revealed truth, ordinary objective certainty implies the existence of satisfactory evidence for its revealed character. Infallibility, as understood and exercised by the Church, prescinds from such evidence. It makes it possible to believe that particular propositions have been revealed in spite of the absence of proof. A number of doctrines, including the Marian dogmas of her immaculate conception and assumption with body and soul into heaven, have been infallibly defined, though there is no satisfactory evidence to prove that they have been revealed; infallibility must substitute for proof.

A priori both ways were open to Jesus to ensure permanent certainty about the gospel: either by endowing his disciples or Church with a charism of infallibility and supplying convincing proof of such endowment; or by merely providing permanent satisfactory evidence for the substance of his gospel. Hence, if the evidence for infallibility is not convincing, we shall be left with the second, more natural, alternative.

The difference has enormous significance for the Church. If the Church depends on ordinary certainties, she is dependent on available evidence and the perception of it. She cannot make herself independent of the extant evidence by overstepping it, as she has done in a number of infallible definitions. Her prior understanding of the revelation or evidence can never be made into an obstacle to the acceptance of newer insights, because it is not the Church's understanding of the revelation that is the final and permanent norm, but the available evidence itself. When nature and weight of available evidence are adequate, it is not impossible to achieve a certainty which may be called absolute or "infallible" (as that 2 + 2 make 4, or that Washington, D.C. is, or has been for years, the capital of the United States), but this "infallibility" is not due to a special charism bestowed by God on certain people, but to the compelling character of the evidence. In other cases the available evidence does not exclude all possibility of error; though, dependent on the nature of the evidence and matter in hand, a careful evaluation by critical educated people may make major errors very exceptional.

Infallibility on the other hand, as claimed and exercised by the Church, does not only allow her to achieve certainties independently from the existence or not of satisfactory evidence; it also leaves no room for errors and changes even in those cases where she exceeded the evidence; infallible teachings, even when based on insufficient evidence, become a permanent norm of belief. Doctrines once solemnly defined on merits on the basis of a 13th or 16th century understanding of bible, tradition, and nature, cannot be re-defined on merits with a 20th century knowledge of bible and history and science. Though some room for revision is left insofar as our understanding of them may have been flawed or they may be shown to be inadequate enunciations of revealed truth, there can be no room for changing their substance.*

The difference is also of fundamental importance in interpreting the data of the New Testament books and of Church history. Papal infallibility was solemnly defined only in 1870 by Vatican I. The infallibility of the Church has never been solemnly defined, though it is clearly taught by Vatican II and referred to in the solemn definition of papal infallibility in Vatican I: "The pope of Rome . . . enjoys that infallibility with which the divine Redeemer wished to endow his Church in deciding doctrines of faith and morals." From the beginning the Apostles and the Church had a conviction of certainty about their knowledge of the gospel, without fully analysing the implications of such a conviction, though

*The embarrassing nature of theology's continued tether to traditional criteria of truth (general consensus, infallibility) is well brought out by Oswald Loretz in his comments (Illusionen nachkonziliarer Ekklesiologie?) on Hans Kueng's latest book *Die Kirche* (The Church) in Theologisch-praktische Quartalschrift, 1967, 4.Heft: "The desperation of theology only reflects that she has not yet succeeded in solving the problem of the autonomy of modern scientific knowledge. Precisely her tie to tradition, to the *consensus omnium,* had to bring about the gravest convulsions when it was attacked in arenas which do not even belong to the area of Revelation (Galilei, Darwin, etc.)... Tests decide about the validity of a principle and no longer this itself. The line of retreat is dictated by tests and not by ecclesiastical authority or theology. As long as theology, in practice and theoretically, takes over uncritically the *consensus omnium* theory, she will be unable to indicate the practical courses of action demanded today. A systematic treatment in the style of *Die Kirche* seems far from able to meet such a demand" (p. 318-9); "We are confronted with the most peculiar fact that in a book of rank as *Die Kirche* there is silence on the methods needed by the Church today in her search for truth and information. May we draw from this the conclusion that present dogmatical method is fundamentally unable to meet the need? The answer must be Yes" (p. 321); "The ecclesiastical magisterium and theology are from Galilei's case to the question of birth control and celibacy exposed to an irresistible process of corrosion of their traditional authority" (p. 332).

they connected it also with Christ's promise of assistance by the Holy Spirit. Only in more recent times was this conviction of certainty interpreted more and more clearly in terms of a charism or prerogative of infallibility. It will be the main burden of our argument to examine whether either the conviction of certainty or the belief in the assistance of the Spirit are proof of the existence of a charism of infallibility as understood in recent times and in the First and Second Vatican Councils.

Theologians admit that our knowledge of the fact of revelation is based on mere historical evidence and certainty; these suffice as a preamble of faith, to make religious or supernatural faith possible and reasonable. If such historical certainty suffices as a preamble of faith where the very foundation of the Christian religion is concerned, a similar certainty must be sufficient also where we are faced with particular revealed truths. For this reason too the question must be squarely faced: Has Christ really provided his Church with a prerogative of infallibility, or has he given his religion a place among the ordinary certainties of mankind, based on good, satisfactory evidence, but without a charism of infallibility?

Before we enter into this question it will be necessary, in order to forestall a number of objections, to consider the relations between certainty, infallibility, and the act of faith. From what seems a wrong analysis of the act of faith there is on the one hand a demand for infallibility, and on the other, under the influence of the form-historical school, a denial of a real historical certainty, and of the need of it, about Christ's transcendent personality and gospel. If this denial could be sustained, it would have fatal consequences for the Christian religion which no amount of theological speculation and whitewash would be able to avert.

III

CERTAINTY, INFALLIBILITY, AND THE ACT OF FAITH

When Jesus demanded faith he ordinarily meant faith as an act of trust in the Father or in him. Underlying such trust, however, is an act of belief in God's existence, truthfulness, mercy and kindness; an intellectual assent therefore to particular realities or truths, which can be considred separately from the act of trust. When he sent his Apostles to make disciples of all nations, to teach them all he had commanded, to be witnesses of what he had said and done, he expected in response also an act of assent to certain truths, even though the final purpose was not a mere increase of religious knowledge, but love and commitment by which man surrenders himself entirely to God and his purposes.

With the act of faith we mean here the willing assent to revealed truth, a religious act of ready submission of will and mind to God revealing himself, specifically different from the act of trust, though often forming with it one complete psychological act of surrender to God.

In contradistinction to religious faith there is also a faith which is a simple intellectual assent based on the knowledge or belief that a person knows what he says and is speaking the truth. Faith in our fellowmen is of this kind. It can exist in regard to a divine revelation as well. The assent is then not a religious surrender of will and mind to God, but only the logical conclusion of a syllogism which has for premisses the facts that God is truthful and has made a revelation. When St. James says that even the devils believe, he refers to this non-religious kind of faith which is merely a kind of knowledge.

Since the act of religious faith, as distinct from trust, is an intellectual assent to truth revealed by God or to God revealing himself, it requires the prior knowledge, or belief, that God has in fact revealed something. Otherwise it is logically impossible to accept something as revealed by God. It is therefore misunderstanding the nature of the act of faith as a religious act, to think that by making the fact of revelation demonstrably certain we destroy or diminish the religious character of the act of faith. On the contrary, religious faith as an act of ready submission of will and mind to the revealing God presupposes knowledge that God has in fact made a revelation. A doubt about the fact of revelation correspondingly weakens the assent or even makes it impossible.

The prior knowledge must be true, that is certain, knowledge, based on sufficient evidence. In the case of Jesus this means that we must have proof that God has really revealed himself, or certain propositions, through him. Such proof can only consist in facts or signs which show that he speaks in the name of God or that God testifies to the truth of what he proclaims. One of those signs may be the very character of the speaker and his message. Their total qualities may be so far above anything man of his own can be or say that we are led to conclude: here is the hand of God. The fact is that Jesus continues to make an unsurpassed impression on the keenest minds. More spectacular signs are the miracles attributed to him.

Since without miraculous signs there would be no means of knowing – apart from a so-called supernatural light of faith which is a pure unverified supposition – that God had confirmed a teaching, there could be no obligation to accept it as coming from him. There would be left truths evident in themselves or an appeal to purely human faith, reasonable to the extent that we can be sure that the speaker has knowledge and is trustworthy. To reject miracles as impossible and yet to postulate a revelation is inconsistent. A true revelation would be an act of special divine intervention as much as any miracle.

Against the attempt to prove by miracles the transcendent character of Jesus and his mission, two main objections are now made. One is that they do not serve the purpose for which they are claimed to be needed, namely to convince people of their supernatural origin. They did not convince many of Jesus' listeners and, as reported, Jesus himself admitted this, for example when he told them, "Truly, truly, I say to you, you seek me, not because you saw signs, but because you ate your fill of the loaves" (Jn 6,26). That they do not convince all people is true enough, but as the evangelists report they did convince many, and Jesus himself appealed to them repeatedly as proof of divine origin. In the very text quoted Jesus evidently scolded his listeners for their lack of understanding and their being moved only by greed. But on this objection more anon.

The other objection raised is of a more abstract nature. It is said that "it is evident to everyone that God cannot abolish the laws of logic or square the circle; but is it philosophically so obvious that we must argue differently in the case of true natural laws? The difficulty is that we infer the natural laws from the facts and then try to prove that certain facts are against natural laws."

That miracles are not simply facts enlarging our knowledge of natural laws is implicitly admitted by the anti-miraculists, by their very refusal to admit their possibility even where they are so well attested as in the case of Jesus. Their argument must therefore fall back on the assertion that the reported miracles would be against nature, on a par with squaring the circle. It may be true that strictly speaking nothing can happen against natural laws. When a dying man is saved by a kidney or heart transplant nothing happens against natural laws. But the transplant is a drastic intervention in the normal run of things. Man intervenes all the time in the ordinary course of events, even when lifting a stone, though not against natural laws, but by making use of them. And he becomes all the time more clever in doing things far beyond what nature does left to itself. What man can do, can be done by other intelligent agents. Without therefore being against nature, why should miracles not be interventions due to an invisible agent? By refusing *a priori* to consider the reported miracles as possible historical events the anti-miraculists implicitly either assert – but how do they prove? – that such facts would be really against nature, on a par with squaring the circle; or, if they are humble enough to admit that their knowledge of nature is too limited to prove such an assertion, they implicitly assert that there can be no invisible free superhuman agent who could make use of the laws of nature in ways (as yet) unknown and inaccessible to man. Since neither assertion has been proved, the *a priori* refusal to consider the possibility of miracles demonstrates a pseudo-philosophical or pseudo-scientific prejudice.

It is argued that "the miraculous content of an event is not and cannot be an object of history." In regard to miracles we must distinguish three things: the observable events, as that Jesus walked on the waters of Lake Gennesaret; their uncommon character; their attribution to the intervention of an invisible power. As observable events miracles are and can be objects of history whose business it is to examine all reports of memorable events, even of such as happened only once and cannot be duplicated or imitated or explained. Our judgement of the uncommon character is based on mankind's present and past experience. Thus, only the explanation of the events does, in fact, transcend history. The *a priori* denial that the events as reported could ever have taken place is an a-historical judgement which decides, before and independently from an impartial historical examination, that the reports are not trustworthy. Inevitably, this deeply colours all later judgements or appraisal of evidence. It is an invitation to prove what has beforehand been decided must be.

After a plane has circled over a lonely undiscovered island, there will be two opinions among the primitive inhabitants: that it was a huge unknown bird; that it was a marvel produced by beings much more intelligent than they. But if the island dwellers have reached a higher state of sophistication, there will probably soon be a third opinion saying that the whole thing was mere phantasy. With their little knowledge of nature the sophisticated ones might even begin to argue that it was against nature, on a par with squaring the circle. This would make them the most "progressive" people on the island. Yet they would be wrong.

The pessimism of the form-historical school about the historical reliability of the New Testament records, which mainly flows from its prejudice against miracles, has also affected some Catholic scholars. This has led them to construct an act of faith which is no longer dependent on the historical evidence that God has spoken. Two of them, in the December 1966 number of *Concilium,* in an article on "Jesus of Nazareth and Christ", write for example: "In this case (of the Christian faith) the interest centers on the message. Does this mean that the facts, through the narration of which the message is transmitted, might never have happened? This is a secondary question, important, but not the most important. . . When we look for historical facts in an historical manner – a perfectly legitimate approach – we put ourselves by the same token outside the approach of faith. And *if we are troubled because the historical investigation yields only a thin harvest* (italics mine), our concern simply shows once again that we are making our faith depend on historically verifiable premisses: it is then not a faith of unconditional *trust* (the authors' italics) but a conclusion drawn from what we consider historical proof." Those who demand prior certainty about the fact that God has spoken, are accused of having "too crude a notion of the relationship between truth and historical knowledge" and as asking "too much of the documents available." After having practically conceded that the New Testament records do not give us certainty, they appear almost disingenuous when they conclude the article with the statement: "There is, of course, also the point – which is beyond the scope of this article – that the trusting act of faith is a truly human act which as such must also be morally justifiable as a free act in the judgement of the human reason. The faith cannot be just an irrational 'leap', which would mean that he who does not dare to take this 'leap' would be just as right as he who does. Historical questions about this historical Jesus of Nazareth from 'outside the faith' are clearly not irrelevant, not insofar as faith as such is concerned but insofar as we are morally responsible for every human decision we make; in this case, the decision to believe."

It is true that the core of Jesus' message is God's love and mercy* and this may commend itself to our belief independently of his miracles. Compared with this central truth, the question of the miracles as mere historical facts, if unrelated to the message, would be a secondary one. But Christ would not be particularly important if he had only proclaimed God's love; others have done the same, though not in equally effective and beguiling ways. His real significance lies in the fact that he is God's love incarnate, that his whole life and especially his passion and death are a personal manifestation – not mere talk or proclamation – of God's love. He had to be God himself to be a visible and personal proof of God's love towards men. And this cannot be known except through miraculous signs proving the truth of his words and status.

But even if Christ were only a messenger from God, not God incarnate, the miracles would be divine testimony to the truth of his message and thus raise it to a certainty superior

*Compared with this and man's reciprocating love, even the new attitude towards man, demanded by Jesus, is secondary. All the same it is of immense practical importance: after the love of God the love of one's fellowmen is the essence of morality. The only possible way of "serving" God is by serving man. Killing, stealing, adultery, etc., are wrong not because God forbids them; God forbids them because they do harm to man – others, oneself, mankind. Nor does he merely demand that we do no harm; he imposes a positive obligation to help others in distress: what is done or left undone to them, is done or left undone to the divine Judge himself (Mt.25, 31-46).

to the one arising from our insight into its own inner reasonableness alone. By denying to the message a solid historical basis in Christ's divinity and miracles, the theory reduces it to what our reason alone can know, and faith in God retains no longer a sure foundation in Christ.

It is an essential feature of the enlightened rational mind that it is unable to give a firm assent, whether of human or divine faith, without satisfactory evidence. If the available documents cannot provide such evidence, if the harvest of historical research is so thin that it leaves a reasonable doubt whether God has indeed revealed himself in Christ, modern scientific mankind will refuse to leap across the gap by an act of unconditional trust. God himself cannot and does not demand that man accept something with greater certainty than the evidence warrants. On insufficient evidence no solid lasting structure can be erected and without it Christianity has no future as a revealed religion.

One of the reasons why it is thought possible to detach faith from certainty is the fact that the evidence is not of the compelling type as that two and two make four. It is the kind that requires good will; i.e., a readiness to consider it with an open and sympathetic mind. This good will is not needed to supply a missing link in the evidence, but to make it possible to give it its due weight.

In the parable of the rich man and Lazarus, Jesus makes Abraham reply: "If they (the rich man's brothers) do not hear Moses and the prophets, neither will they be convinced if some one should rise from the dead." He refers to the well-known ability of man to close his mind against what he does not wish to be true, which is only the counterpart of his talent for accepting wishes as facts. Man faces Christ's claims already conditioned by convictions and emotions that predispose him for belief or disbelief. Prior judgements are rarely a sign of bad will, but man is put to the test when confronted with new facts.

Another reason which seems to make it possible to detach faith from prior certainty about the fact of revelation is that most people have faith without evidence sufficient in itself. Most Christians accept Christ in reliance on others. If their evidence is better than that on which Muslims accept Mohammed's words or Hindus the Vedas, it is so only at greater depth to which they do not penetrate. Since faith is attainable by the majority of Christians without valid evidence, it is possible to conclude that such evidence is not necessary for the Christian faith. Yet such conclusion would be wrong. Though not required for the mass of believers, valid evidence is absolutely needed to hold the allegiance of the educated critical minority that in the long run determines the beliefs of a more advanced society.

Against this analysis of the situation; i.e., of the need of satisfactory evidence as a foundation for the act of faith, a twofold attack is mounted, from opposite directions.

One objects, with the authors quoted from *Concilium,* that if we base the knowledge of the fact and contents of revelation on evidence, we destroy the character of the act of faith; this cannot be based on evidence, but only on "unconditional trust" in God. Religious, supernatural faith would be reduced to an act of human knowledge and deprived both of its religious nature and of its absolute certainty which is based on God. The authors appear to suggest that the less sure we are of the fact of revelation the more our trust will be truly "unconditional", as apparently it ought to be.

As noted already, a clear distinction must be made between the knowledge that God has spoken and the subsequent religious act of faith which is an assent to what he has revealed out of a ready submission of will and mind to him. For religious faith the first act is only of a preliminary character, but it must precede to make the other possible and supply it with its subject matter. We cannot reasonably give a firm assent to propositions as revealed, unless we are first sure that God has in fact revealed them. Far from standing in the way of the second act, it is what makes the second act fully possible and reasonable. It is true that man is able to accept things without sufficient reason and to achieve certainties on invalid grounds, but this is part of his mental weakness, not a manifestation of his strength. Man in his full mental stature accepts with certainty only what is evident, what he perceives to be true. To demand of him that he submit himself to a revelation of God, or a truth as revealed by God, without evidence to show that God has actually made the revelation, is to demand of him that he abdicate his intelligence and cease to be fully reasonable. Certainty about the fact of revelation is the one condition we can safely put, and must put, to be true to our rational God-given nature.

Though we must distinguish between the preliminary knowledge of the fact of revelation and the subsequent act of religious assent, these two acts belong together as one complete act of judgement and assent. In its perfection the complete act has a double ground of certainty: the morally certain knowledge, based on trustworthy testimony, of the fact of revelation, and the absolute certainty due to God's truthfulness. But Christians often wrongly believe that a particular proposition has been revealed and give their assent to it out of a ready submission to God. On finding out their mistake they must withdraw their assent of faith. This does not mean that they withdraw their faith in God or their total readiness to submit to him. There is no failure in the act of faith as a religious act, neither on the part of man nor on the part of God. The failure is only in the preliminary knowledge. It would be absurd to continue the religious assent even after it has become known that a proposition has not been revealed.

The religious elements of the act of faith are verified whether a proposition to which assent is given has actually been revealed or not. But the world has no reward for good intentions. If a man gives a religious assent of faith to a proposition he mistakes for revealed, he is in error and will suffer the consequences of his error. It is, therefore, not enough to have the right attitude of faith to God, we must also make sure that what we give assent to has really been revealed. In the totality of the act of assent each has its own value, the religious submission to God and the proposition to which assent is given. The first retains its religious value, even if we have to abandon the second.

The other objection to the analysis proposed above proceeds from an opposite direction. It asserts that in order to be able to make an act of faith we must have infallible certainty that God has revealed a proposition. If we have no infallible certainty, we may be mistaken. But the act of faith must be absolute and no mistake can be allowed to enter it.

Here an attempt is made to introduce the absolute character which faith has as a religious act into the act of knowledge that precedes it. The absoluteness of certainty which in the act of faith is only due to God being the infinite truth and to man's readiness to submit to him, is here made an attribute of our knowledge about the fact of revelation. But this knowledge can never be absolute. It is human knowledge, based on human testimony, apprehended in a human manner. The attempt to introduce infallible certainty into this knowledge is futile. Our knowledge that a revelation has taken place and about its contents, including the claim to infallibility or its application to particular doctrines, are all based on acts of ordinary, non-infallible, human judgements. The demand for infallibility is, therefore, based on a wrong notion of the act of faith and of where the nature lies of its absoluteness.

Only insofar as an act of faith implies an assent to God's word and the will to submit to him must it be absolute. There can be no valid reasons to withdraw these. But man can maintain this willing faith in God also when he withholds an act of assent because he is convinced that a revelation has not taken place or doubts if it has. On the other hand the religious elements of faith are activated in the very common case when a believer gives religious assent to a doctrine – or, in the case of a member of a non-revealed religion, to a religion – which he mistakes for revealed. It is obvious that whenever it is found that the doctrine, or religion, was after all not revealed, the assent of faith already given must be withdrawn. This withdrawal of assent only affects the particular doctrine or religion, not man's attitude towards God.

The reasons given by Vatican I requiring man's total obedience of intellect and will to God in faith are his total dependence on him as his Creator and Lord and the dependence of his created intellect on uncreated truth. But these are not engaged in the preliminary judgement man has to make about whether a particular doctrine or proposed revelation does come from God. A wrong judgement or a change of opinion on this preliminary question does not affect man's readiness to submit to God.

Psychologically it is easy enough for most people to adhere with full assent to particular doctrines as revealed without attention to the value of the evidence advanced for their revealed character. This, however, does not enhance the act of faith, only reduces its character as a completely reasonable human act of assent.

It is wrong to think that the cause of true religion is served – especially for mankind as a whole – by diminution of attention to evidence or by accepting propositions with greater certainty than the evidence warrants. There can be no obligation to make the act of faith as an assent stronger by refusing to remain aware, in the totality of the act of assent, that our knowledge of the fact of revelation is only one of moral certainty. In particular propositions this certainty is further reduced, since there is not the same weight of concurring evidence for each individual proposition as there is for the fact of revelation as a whole. Hence, for example, we are more certain that Christ is a messenger from God than we are of his divinity. The weight of proof for the first is much heavier than for the second. This does not mean that the second is doubtful. We are also historically more certain of Napoleon and Hitler than of the battle of Austerlitz or the infamy of Auschwitz, but no one can reasonably doubt the two latter events.

Infallibility as an attempt to make everything equally, infallibly sure is failing in its purpose. On the other hand it is illusory to expect that Christianity can survive as a revealed religion, or even as a major moral force, on the strength of an act of so-called unconditional trust, without really valid historical evidence for Jesus' transcendent personality and mission.

IV

CERTAINTY AND THE GOSPELS

A religious community is in need of certainty, of a certainty based on valid evidence. Even infallibility cannot do away with the need of evidence; to be acceptable it must be based on solid proof. At least those of good will who are educated and critical, who make a study of religion and can assess evidence, must be convinced on good grounds that its claims are true. They hold the key of knowledge for a whole community. Without valid evidence the convictions of the educated will be gradually eroded, and then abandoned by them and by the rest of the people. The need for evidence increases with the progress in general knowledge and maturity of a society. Modern learned man refuses to hold his convictions by infection or luck.* He demands proof. Religious foundations which seem good enough to a primitive, pre-scientific society will not suffice unless they prove really valid.

Christianity has always claimed to be based on a historical personality and events. For us the validity of the claim depends in practice on the historical trustworthiness of the gospels and other New Testament books, corroborated by early Christian history and references in non-Christian

*The Germans say: Der Mensch denkt durch Ansteckung; Denken ist Gluecksache: Man thinks by infection; thinking is a matter of luck.

authors, and more especially on the miraculous events in Jesus' life. If these foundations are not tenable, we are left with no more than the proclamation of a message or belief, surrounded by a mass of legends, with no historical evidence that it is true.

The dominant recent school of bible criticism which takes a very pessimistic view of the trustworthiness of the bible is the form-historical school whose dominant figures, Dibelius, Bultmann, and Schmidt, published their first works around 1920. In his book, *Jesus*, published in 1926, Bultmann remarks: "It is quite clear that he (Jesus) caused a historical movement, of which the Palestinian Church formed the first tangible stage. But how far the Church preserved an objectively true picture about him and his preaching, is a different question. For those who are interested in the personality of Jesus, the situation is depressive if not desperate; for us this question (of historicity) has no more than trivial importance." Their interest centers around the "kerygmatic Christ", Christ as preached by the first Christians, who must lead us to adopt an existential attitude towards life and to accept his proclamation as a call to personal conversion and engagement. Modern man, they say, cannot accept the supernatural events recorded in the gospels. Nor does he need do violence to his reason by believing them. They are only part of the ancient form of the message, understandable within the ancient concept of the world which saw everywhere the working of supernatural powers. For modern man the ancient form becomes an obstacle to the understanding of the message itself. To make this accessible to him we have to strip the bible of all its mythical, supernatural elements. The preaching of the New Testament was done in terms of that age. Those terms have become meaningless to us. But the message itself, the glad tidings, God's gesture calling us to faith and obedience, remains valid for us today.

It is not the object of this little thesis to enter into the controversy around the form-historical school, but in dealing with the need of certainty as a basis of the Christian faith, some observations are appropriate which seem to prove the need of a much more positive attitude towards the historical trustworthiness of the gospel accounts.

It is easy enough to see why modern man is shy of miracles. Until recently the knowledge of the workings of natural causes was very limited. Everything out of the ordinary, of which the causes were not known, was attributed to the working of supernatural powers. Man has learned. He has done away with nearly all the old mysteries. He is confident that those which remain will also yield to his understanding. In his experience miracles do not happen. It is easy to conclude that miracles never happened and cannot happen. Neither conclusion, however, is scientific: that they cannot happen is a philosophical, not a scientific, statement; that they never happened is a historical one. In a theistic system the first seems obviously absurd; on the basis of history the second statement runs in the face of extremely strong evidence, and this evidence is particularly strong in the case of Jesus.

One valid proof against prejudice is an appeal to facts, another an appeal to the absurd conclusions to which it leads. There are good reasons to believe that the authors of the gospels intended to write a factual, reliable account of the events around Jesus. The prologue of St. Luke's gospel, the repeated appeal to first-hand testimony, to what they have seen and heard, and other factors prove this. Addressing their accounts in the main to a Greek audience it is also reasonable to assume that the evangelists conformed as far as possible to their notions of historical truthfulness. Where the form-historical school runs directly counter to human experience is in its claim that Christ's disciples had only vague, uncertain memories to go by when decades later they wrote their memories down. How absurd this is, is evident from the normal experience of old people with fairly good memories. We are fortunate in having plenty of them around whom we can ask. Many have clear recollections about all the major things that happened to them, with many details, forty, fifty and even seventy years before. The main lacuna in their memories is the element of time and therefore of sequence. Autobiographies of many writers demonstrate the same tenacity of memory. Yet in the case of most people the memories are of small events, of little importance even to themselves. The very dedication and willingness to accept every hardship, even death, displayed by Jesus' disciples, prove that their memories were of events that they considered of extreme importance to themselves and others. To say that the memories of all of them had become vague and unreliable as to their major experiences, after less than fifty years, is absurd; the theory is explicable only because of the wrongness of the prejudice from which it started. It runs against a very common and demonstrable fact of human experience.

There is another fact of common human behaviour. The disciples were all literate. At an early stage of their association with Jesus they were sent out to preach and, soon after, they were told that they were to be witnesses of Jesus and his message to all nations. They must have reminisced as people do who share great memories. They must have done so especially because to pass them on had become their life's task. Soon they must have noticed that some details were getting blurred, that even some major events and teachings were no longer so readily recallable to some of them. What do people do in such circumstances, when they have to retain those memories. They begin to take notes, more or less extensive ones, to record what seems to them important or interesting. How can we expect Jesus' disciples to have done otherwise? Those with a habit of writing, a Matthew, a John, must have begun early. Others may have been content for a longer time to rely on their vivid recollections, till they perhaps too felt that they were slipping. Again others, with less good memories, must have started to take or borrow notes as soon as they had to be on their own. These are normal, obvious ways of reacting of people in the circumstances in which the disciples found themselves. On all these points the form-historical school condemns itself by running against common psychological facts.

A demand creates a supply, at least when it can be met easily. Very soon after Pentecost the Apostles and other disciples spread out to preach the gospel outside Jerusalem and within a decade it had begun to spread over the Roman empire. Everywhere disciples were appointed to carry on the work of preaching. Not being eye- and earwitnesses they must have been anxious to have some reliable permanent record of the gospel events. Luke tells us that many had written already before him. How can we doubt it? The further the preaching spread, and the less access preachers and listeners had to the original witnesses, the more they demanded and came to rely on records written or acknowledged by them as faithful to the gospel message and events. It must have been to serve the need of the preachers and of those who had no access to the original witnesses that most accounts were written. (We have the very early testimony of St. Justin Martyr, in his *Apologia* of about 150 A.D., that it was a well-established custom in Christian assemblies to read the gospels. The custom must have been started long before.)

There is another good reason for rejecting the pessimism of the Formgeschichte about the historicity of the major contents of the gospel records. Due to official time being an artificial reckoner superimposed on the flow of events, the elements of time and sequence are a weak spot in our memories. In our recollections time retains only a hold on us if it connects events with each other, causally or otherwise, and the connection is recognized. Happenings and instructions which are complete in themselves, not receiving any further light or importance from their temporal setting, are usually remembered without it. It is for this reason that except in the passion narratives the gospels do not provide us with a historical, time-ordered sequence of Jesus' public life, but with loose episodes artificially strung together. The loose pieces were, moreover, coloured by their use in teaching and, of course, contained the kind of inaccuracies and contradictions common to all human observations, recollections and reports. To conclude from these facts that the information contained in them is substantially unreliable is to pronounce the same verdict on all our recollections; they are all subject to the same laws of timeless suspension, inaccuracies and adaptation to later needs. Experience proves such a verdict wrong. Besides, it is generally admitted by bible scholars that the hundreds of parables, figures of speech, symbols (mashl/mathla), etc., found in the gospels, with the exception perhaps of a couple of proverbial sayings, are certainly to be attributed to Jesus himself. Even the substantial form of the parables, with their inimitable clarity and economy of line, are certainly Jesus' own, though applications and endings have suffered from adaptation to different later needs. The striking controversial pieces, too, and the traps he set and sprung, as well as teachings going against strong common convictions and national feelings, are unmistakably genuine. The main reason to account for the tenacity with which all these parts were remembered with substantial fidelity is their vivid, striking, original character which impressed them much more deeply on the memory of the witnesses than mere abstract teaching could have done. But doesn't the same apply – even more so – to the more striking and isolated of his miracles? Whenever, as the evangelists narrate repeatedly, he cured all the many sick brought to him, it must have been impossible after some time to recall the individual cures. But when a miracle happened in isolation or was of a particularly uncommon character or was connected with a fascinating instruction or dispute, was it not to be expected that these would remain firmly implanted in the memory of the witnesses? Surely it is not their being remembered as isolated episodes, nor their being used for purposes of later instruction, that can be adduced as valid reasons for doubting their genuineness as historical events.

The importance of their use in later preaching must not be exaggerated as a cause for inducing changes in the remembered material. Jesus' whole life had but one purpose; to be a revelation of God. By preaching and explaining exactly what happened the disciples passed on the essential message contained in it. To distort his life or words easily meant to distort the message. Some parables addressed to

Jesus' adversaries were later given a different slant to adapt them to another audience, but most sayings and the miracles, which in the main had no other purpose than to prove God's love and Jesus' divine mission, had only to be reported faithfully to continue to serve their evangelical purpose, Jesus' own and that of the early Church. Most events and even instructions recorded are so complete or rounded-off in themselves and pared to the bone that though lessons may be drawn from them for further instruction, they themselves remain unaffected by such application to later use. Besides, from the very purpose they set themselves the evangelists seem to have done their best to place Jesus' teachings and deeds within their original setting or context, whenever this helped to elucidate their meaning. This meant, whenever the teaching or event was remembered together with its setting precisely because it received more light from it.

Admitting that the preaching was done in terms of that age, it must be noted how little of Jesus' message lost its freshness and intelligibility for us. From his custom to clothe his teaching with parables, metaphors, figures of speech, we may rightly deduce with Joachim Jeremias that these have preserved the whole essence of his message. Though taken from a traditional agrarian society, which is very different from the industrialized society of our modern cities, there are surprisingly few parables, etc. that cannot be understood in their essence without difficulty by ordinary literate city-dwellers of today. It will be hard to find even a dozen parables and prominent figures of speech which are not much more easily understood by the great majority of modern westerners than the innards of a t.v. set, a combustion engine, or a telephone. It is not our ability to understand the terms or major contents of Jesus' message that has been lost, but only a number of primitive views of his listeners, especially of the working of God's providence, to which Jesus accommodated himself. We know that special divine interventions are not common daily occurrences; that God does not throw shafts of lightning or beat the drums of thunder, nor enter into the chain of earthly causes to make the sun shine and the rain fall, to send sickness and health, life and death. But if we conclude from this that miracles cannot and do not happen, we jump to scientifically unwarranted conclusions. God and his intentions and range of power are not subject to experiment by scientists in their laboratories. Their tests tell us nothing of what he can or will do. It is therefore unscientific to subordinate the search for historical truth entirely to the unproven postulate that miracles cannot happen.

If the gospels are judged without prejudice about the possibility or not of miracles, they emerge as belonging to the most reliable contemporary writings we have of ancient times. On a fraction of their testimony we build most of our certainties of Greek and Roman history. When faced with narratives of miracles it is, of course, necessary to enquire with extra care whether there are good reasons to believe that the authors have been mistaken or that the miracle stories were composed as a literary device.* This does not weaken the main body of those stories that are an integral part of the gospels and have all the characteristics of happenings easily observed and faithfully reported. Rejecting them out of hand, on a philosophical or scientistic prejudice, has forced the Formgeschichte to untenable conclusions. The records themselves and the character of the writers show up the absurdities and contradictions into which prejudice gets critics involved.

*Bible scholars tend to believe that the stories about Jesus' infancy were fabricated to express the fulfilment in him of Old Testament prophecies and expectations. In a few cases the so-called prophecies are so far-fetched that one is almost forced to believe that the story is primary and the prophecy secondary, as when Matthew speaks of the fulfilment of the prophecies: "Out of Egypt have I called my son"; "He shall be called a Nazarene". The length of time that had passed is alone not a sufficient reason for rejecting the historicity of the infancy stories, since Mary and almost certainly other participants lived until long after the Apostles started their preaching.

V

THE EVIDENCE: MORE GENERAL OBSERVATIONS

Christianity always claimed to be based on solid evidence, on the first-hand and trustworthy witness of the Apostles and early disciples which was written down when their memories were fresh. It is this testimony that gives us our certainty about Christ, his divine mission and message. Though we have no "infallible certainty" about the major contents of those writings, we have the same certainty the early Christians had, since we have before us the same first-hand witness. In the case of other books from antiquity scholars rarely have difficulty in arriving at a consensus about their meaning, even when there is question not of ordinary narratives and statements, but of philosophical writings. For many centuries a similar unanimity of view existed among Christians about the main contents of the gospels and other New Testament Scriptures. This consensus was achieved without appeal to infallibility; it preceded it. On some questions it had been arrived at after a prolonged study and dispute on what the Scriptures taught, as in the case of the Trinity and the nature of Christ. The decisions of the ecumenical councils were an expression of the fact that the discussions had reached their final stage and that the conclusions commended themselves as convincing to the great majority of bishops and scholars in the Church. The solemn definitions, accepted by the Church at large, set the matter at rest and produced a consensus among the great majority of Christians that lasted till long after the East-West schism and the Reformation and, in fact, is almost intact even today among Christians believing in a divine revelation. The definitions were appealed to as proof of certainty and those who thereafter set up an opinion contrary to the accepted ones had the Church, and presumption, against them. The ecumenical councils were certain that they taught the truth, but this certainty was based in the first place on the conviction that the evidence from Scripture was compelling; that is on biblical and objective, not on subjective, grounds.

Though the Fathers of the ecumenical councils seem to have decided the controversies on objective grounds, that is, on what the biblical texts proved to them, they believed also that they were guided by the Holy Spirit in their final decisions. In their more primitive view of how God intervenes in his creation, a view that also permeates the bible, they could not think differently. If we analyse the main reasons that induced the majority of Christians to accept the council decisions we probably find these three: the strength of the arguments from Scripture which led the Council Fathers to their decisions in the first place; the readiness of men to accept the opinion of scholars and experts (as today we accept the findings of congresses of scientists); and the belief that the Spirit guides the Church in such decisions. Since the latter conviction was in accord with the common view of the working of divine providence and based on the bible as understood from the beginning, it is probable that soon attention was almost only paid to the latter reason; but this does not invalidate the other two. In a non-infallibilist view of things, the real weight will be shifted back to the first reason, the validity of the scriptural proof, and to the second insofar as a consensus of responsible scholars and thinkers gives a strong presumption of truth. In this view, therefore, doctrinal decisions of Councils do not derive their final authority from the ecumenical character of the Councils, nor from the fact that these have been summoned or endorsed by a pope, nor from a special preservation from error by the

Spirit, but from the validity of the evidence on which they are based. (We have begun to experience today that when council decisions as traditionally understood come into conflict with newer knowledge, theologians move heaven and earth to make room for newer interpretations that will be in accord with the newer evidence. This portends that council definitions will only survive insofar as they are based on valid grounds.)

Whilst preserving from the outset the consensus with the Mother Church on the main truths clearly contained in the gospels, the Reformation threw out a challenge to her on a number of other beliefs. In the dispute that arose and spread over increasingly wider areas, the Reformers rejected the appeal of the Catholic Church to non-biblical evidence, that is, to her own consciousness of certainty or, with other words, to her teaching authority and its traditions. This was the first major factor responsible for the breakdown of unanimity among western Christians. In the course of time the Church's certainties had grown beyond those contained in or demonstrable from the New Testament books; she had developed many certainties for which she could produce no proof. The only proof was she herself, her conviction of certainty or her traditions. This major factor leading to the breakdown of the consensus has nothing to do with the question whether unanimity can be achieved and retained on what the New Testament teaches about Christ and his gospel. The Church had left the bible as sole foundation and added another in order to justify doctrines or convictions that could not be demonstrated from the bible. On the face of it, and independently from the validity of the Church's claim, the Reformers had a very good case. Only if the Church's claim can be substantiated, were the Reformers fundamentally wrong, though they were even then right on many points of detail, since many views accepted by the Church were, as understood, neither infallible nor true.

The second major factor responsible for the breakdown of unanimity was the bitterly antagonistic spirit that soon animated the leading Reformers. It introduced a number of divisive elements into the new movement, away from the Mother Church, but also away from one another and from a united effort to understand the bible. A similar authority as seemed to be claimed by Luther was usurped by an increasing number of people. The popularity of bible reading only added to the confusion. Many began to claim an enlightenment by the Spirit, whether in interpreting the bible or for independent personal ideas, without any reference to the rest of the community of believers. The sense of Church was lost, which is an integral part of Christ's work. The gospel can be understood properly only by a common effort, that is, within the Church and by the Church. When the will to unity was lost and each felt free to go his own way, the understanding of the gospel had to suffer. Christ wishes all his disciples to stay together and solve unitedly, under the spiritual leadership instituted by him, whatever problems arise. To judge about the contents of the bible is the task of the whole Church in which the specialized knowledge of scholars and mystics is balanced by the common sense of others. Any development in understanding has to appeal to the good sense of the community and prove its validity by eventually gaining more general acceptance. Though newer insights, as all new ideas, begin with one man or a few, it is the community which is the final judge of their soundness. A determination to remain united in one Church is an essential demand Jesus makes of his followers; it supposes a spirit of honesty, detachment, and accommodation in the search for truth.

It was an appeal to the Holy Spirit that was responsible for the breakdown of unanimity; on the part of the Catholic Church an appeal to him as guarantee of truth independently from biblical evidence; in the case of the Protestants an appeal to him independently from the Church, the community of Christ's followers. Each in its own way undermined the authority and religious efficacy of the New Testament; the Catholic Church by denying that it can give us assured knowledge or by ranking extra-biblical traditions on a par with the bible and, consequently, by diminishing its excelling role as witness in favour of the living magisterium, with the catechism replacing the bible; the churches of the Reformation by conceding to individual readers too much competence and authority to interpret it in independence of the rest of the Christian community, thus causing an increasing dissent and doubt about its contents.

In the case of other books from antiquity, a study by a larger number of qualified scholars practically assures certainty and unanimity about their contents. What little islands of incomprehension remain are due to the difficulty of subject matter or language. There is no reason to believe that a study based on the same canons of research and interpretation will not lead among Christians of good will to a renewed consensus about the essential contents of the gospels. In the past it was not the magisterium that led to unanimity, but, on the contrary, study and discussion led to views that were generally accepted, also by the magisterium. A new consensus is building up today. Remaining differences of opinion are usually due to dogmatic positions inherited from the past. Unanimity of view is the normal result of detached scholarship. But there will always be minority groups of people who follow their own fancies.

It was long after the Reformation that a combination of factors led to a total breakdown which affected the very foundations of Christianity, including its trinitarian and christological beliefs. The schism in western christendom was one factor that prepared the way. The individualistic principle, with its divisive consequences, was another. Probably more important than even these was belief in a divine inspiration and inerrancy of the bible combined with biblical literalism. This claimed that every text and phrase of the bible, understood in its literal sense, was divinely inspired and free from error. The spirit of scientific enquiry, which had received a strong impetus in the Renaissance and re-asserted itself once the religious fervour of Reformation and Counter-Reformation had ebbed away, found it increasingly easy to show that the bible, interpreted literally, was full of errors and contradictions. Eventually this destroyed many people's faith in the bible as a whole and in the Christian religion built on it. If anything, this goes to show that an appeal to infallibility alone, without proper evidence or, worse, against evidence, will not preserve a consensus, but lead inevitably to its breakdown. Already the breaching of traditional views on the meaning and extent of infallibility has set in over a broad front, so that the present standpoint of some leading theologians on infallibility is as different from the traditional one as modern exegesis is from biblical literalism.

The principles of a scientific interpretation of the bible, accepted today by nearly all major churches, have overcome the difficulties associated with the former literal interpretation. They also laid the basis for a far-reaching consensus on the meaning of the bible. But alongside this the rationalistic virus, which rejects the historicity of all miraculous accounts and supernatural claims in the gospels, remains very active. Here lies the real chasm dividing believing Christians from others in what was once christendom. Compared with it all other divisions must be considered secondary, though some are not unimportant. There are the biblical literalists and those who accept scientific principles of bible interpretation; those who do and those who do not believe in a divine inspiration and inerrancy of the bible; those who believe that the gospels contain with sufficient clarity all the essentials of Christ's revelation and those who believe that other essentials, not demonstrable from the bible alone, have been preserved with the aid of an oral tradition under a special guidance of the Spirit; those who give almost equal weight to the books of Old and New Testament and those who find the essence of Christianity in the gospels and other New Testament books, etc.

For the purposes of the thesis we shall accept that the historical writings of the New Testament are authentic and trustworthy records of the main events and message of the gospel. If we avoid the three factors mentioned above, which led to disagreement about the contents of these records, we obtain certainty and unanimity on the main facts. They are obtained in the same way as mankind achieves them about other historical facts, by authentic, clear, and reliable records.

We must therefore accept the substance of the Protestant thesis that the bible gives us reliable, certain knowledge of at least the main gospel events and teachings. In fact, the Church has always accepted this. She has always appealed to the bible to prove the truth of Christ and his gospel to educated non-Christian. She has appealed to it to demonstrate the truth of doctrines that were in fact clearly contained in the bible. She also appeals to it when she tries to prove her claim to infallibility. Yet in spite of all this she has refused to accept the Protestant thesis that the bible alone suffices for the faith.

There is no doubt that Christ commanded his disciples to teach. The need of a body of teachers is permanent. No book alone can reach all people or be understood properly by all readers. Until relatively recent years the majority of people in most countries was illiterate. Besides, even now, most people are unable or unwilling to take the trouble to read or understand a book. It is only a living, permanent magisterium that can pass on Christ's revelation to all people. The situation is no different in the field of secular knowledge. Our schools do not just teach children to read and then hand them the appropriate books to acquire the necessary knowledge. Oral teaching has to supplement the written word. It will be no different when in a future time most teaching will be done with the help of television. In this sense, therefore, the bible is not enough. Christ trained a body of teachers and commissioned them to teach the whole world. This implies the passing on of the same task to others who also have to be trained. The bible is also not enough because, as noted, it can be understood only within the Church by a common effort to understand and live it.

The question therefore is not whether a teaching body or Church is needed or not, but what the contents must be of the teaching. The Protestant churches claim that the bible contains all necessary revealed truth with sufficient clarity; the Catholic Church claims that there is other revealed truth that cannot be known with certainty from the bible. According to her, the living magisterium is an independent judge of the contents of its own teachings.

We must first deal briefly with the traditional Catholic objections to the Protestant position. There is nothing in the bible to show that it alone is the norm of faith. It is not even possible to show from the New Testament books, apart from a remark by St. Peter about St. Paul's writings, that there is such a thing as New Testament Scriptures. Their value as such depends therefore entirely on the oral tradition. It is also impossible to determine, on the basis of the bible, which books belong to the Scriptures of the New Testament. Moreover, the canon or list of New Testament books was established quite late. As far as we know Irenaeus was the first to try to establish it. One would therefore have to admit that at least till then the oral preaching was the norm of faith. Did it change later? There is no proof for that. For centuries the living magisterium of the Church was the norm of faith. Did the Church err during all those centuries? Finally – an objection with which we have dealt sufficiently – readers cannot find out for themselves what to believe, as is shown by the many divisions of the churches of the Reformation.

Much has already been said that contains an answer to the objections raised, but a short reply to the major ones seems necessary.

The bible never existed in a vacuum. It originated and continued to exist and live in the community of Christ's disciples. The authenticity and authority of its books depended on the fact that they either originated with the Apostles or were endorsed by them, and that this fact was recognized by the Christian community, for each component part, in an ever widening circle. The bible was therefore never fully self-establishing and even today its authority cannot be isolated from its apostolic origins and from all those factors that help establish its authenticity and reliability. It is the Christian community which inherited it and passes it on to its members and to the world and which is the best guarantee of a right understanding of it. In the following remarks this must not be lost sight of.

For the Scriptures to be the foundation or norm of faith it is not necessary for them expressly to mention it. They are the norm of faith because they are, and can be proved to be, authentic, trustworthy, records of what Jesus said and did. Even if they were to vouch for the existence of all the New Testament books, through cross-references, these would not be valid simply because they are in the bible, but because the bible is authentic and reliable.

Though the living magisterium was prior in time to the New Testament books, wrote them, and guaranteed their authenticity, this is only true for the Apostles themselves. As officially commissioned witnesses they either wrote the books or authenticated their conformity with the facts. The New Testament books are essentially the apostolic witness in written form. The oral and written apostolic testimony are substantially of equal value; they were two different expressions of the same apostolic "ministry of the word" or magisterium. Whilst each had its own peculiar advantages, the question of which was more authoritative than the other did not arise. Yet the written witness had over the oral one the considerable advantages of permanence, a wider dissemination in place and time, the presentation of the whole substance in easily accessible form, and more careful editing.

The magisterium of later times, which does not consist of eye- and earwitnesses, does not inherit the Apostles' authority over the New Testament books. On the contrary, it depends on them for proof of its own authenticity and legitimacy. For us the authority of the present magisterium is based on the bible, not vice versa. It is only through the bible that we know that Christ trained a body of disciples and commanded them to teach all nations. Besides, because it is the authoritative, original witness of the Apostles themselves about Christ, the bible is superior to the derived teaching about him of the later magisterium. It constitutes for that teaching the source and norm. The task of the later magisterium is essentially to pass on and explain and apply the contents of the original apostolic witness; its relation to it can only be one of subordination and service.

Even in the case of the Apostles, their verdict on the authenticity of the New Testament books was not independent from the character of those books, but on the contrary a recognition on their part that they were an expression of the original witness or in conformity with it. Not all these writings were equally essential to the Church or equally well-known in the beginning. Some of them, including probably all the gospels, the Acts, and the major epistles of St. Paul, were already widely spread and recognized as authentic during the life-time of the Apostles. When later the question of the authenticity of the others was expressly raised in the Church, it took time to come to a consensus, but the reason why they were accepted as such must have been good evidence that they originated with the Apostles or had their approval. In coming to this verdict the recognition of their accord with the books already generally accepted probably played a major part. It was ultimately, also in their case, these writings themselves, their inherent authenticity, which determined their acceptance into the canon of New Testament books.

There was of course a transition from reliance on oral tradition to reliance on the Scriptures. This transition came very soon. The original witnesses could appeal to what they had personally heard and seen. Their companions and others within visiting distance could still verify their memories and preaching by an appeal to the Apostles personally. Soon the great majority of preachers, far from them in place or time, had probably only a few major facts and truths from second-hand or distant hearsay, or others perhaps had scraps of notes to go by; they therefore started to rely on the written apostolic witness as soon as it became available. For them the Scriptures soon became the only really trustworthy testimony. In the prologue Luke gives this as reason for writing his gospel: "to write an orderly account for you, most excellent Theophilus, that you may know the truth concerning the things of which you have been informed," Lk. 1, 1-4.

Compared with the bible, the living magisterium is a much less satisfactory norm of faith than may at first sight appear. The great majority of Church members are only confronted with the fallible teaching of parents, parish clergy, and catechists. They have no way of knowing what is really infallible and accept all they are taught with equal faith. Even expert theologians can rarely be certain whether, apart from the major doctrines clearly contained in the New Testament records, other doctrines generally taught by the Church do, as understood, really fulfill all the conditions required for infallibility. As will be shown in a later chapter, quite a number of doctrines accepted for centuries as certain and infallible, had later to be abandoned, corrected, or explained, and only elaborate historical research, conducted and verifiable by a few, can prove that in these cases the conditions for infallibility of the ordinary magisterium were after all not fulfilled. The Church cannot do without the magisterium, but the ultimate source of certainty is hardly the intricate investigations required to prove that in particular doctrines all the conditions for infallibility are really met. Compared with this, the recognition by the community and its scholars that propositions are clearly part of Christ's gospel as preserved for us in the New Testament books, seems a much more obvious ground for certainty. It has in fact been considered sufficient for a number of major revealed truths which therefore were never solemnly defined.

There seem to be good *a priori* reasons to believe with the churches of the Reformation that the Scriptures, especially the four gospels, do actually contain clearly all the essentials of Christ's revelation.

The Apostles were commissioned by Jesus to teach all he had commanded, to all nations. In the beginning they must have relied on their memories and probably on some notes they had taken or took soon after. But spreading out, and with the passage of time, it must have become apparent to them that not only they themselves to some extent, but especially the teachers appointed by them in various places, could not be relied upon to remember all the major features of Christ's life and doctrine. More particularly was it impossible for the new teachers to have a vivid picture of the personality of Jesus and the uniqueness of his teachings. To make sure that the gospel with a sufficient * number of examples of his miracles and instructions would reach all and retain its unique substance, it had to be given a permanent form in authentic written accounts. Even if Jesus did not tell them to write down their testimony, the facts themselves must have convinced the Apostles that their task could not be carried out without it. Expressly written with the intention to give the readers and the Church at large a reliable and substantially complete picture of Jesus and his gospel, their accounts must clearly** contain all that is essential, supplemented by many secondary details that help give a vivid picture of his personality and doctrine and their impact on his audience. As we have four such reports, written one after the other, it is unlikely that later evangelists did not supplement any essential feature earlier writers might have inadvertently omitted. This seems the obvious conclusion to be drawn from the intention of the authors and from the task that had been entrusted to them.

*Towards the end of his gospel St. John writes, "Jesus did many other signs in the presence of his disciples, which are not written in this book; but these are written that you may believe that Jesus is the Christ, the Son of God, and that believing you may have life in his name," Jn.20,30-31. It was only necessary to write down a sufficient number of miraculous signs to prove Jesus' character and mission. Similarly it was necessary to record a number of his instructions, not only to give the substance of his teaching, but also to demonstrate that "no man ever spoke like this man", Jn. 7,46. All this could not have been done and preserved by oral teaching alone.

**There are of course degrees of clarity. The christological and trinitarian controversies arose also because on these points the records were, at first sight, not so clear as to exclude all possibility of doubt.

The Acts and Epistles confirm what the gospels teach about Jesus without, it seems, adding anything to the substance of it. We meet in them the Apostles carrying out their task and applying Jesus' teaching to particular stituations. Later, in the early Church, when doubts or controversies arise, the appeal is to the Scriptures and to what little an oral tradition could initially still add. Soon the Scriptures had become the only trustworthy source of information about Jesus and his message. When Origen states (*De princ.*, 1, pracf.3) that the Apostles have with great clarity passed on ("manifestissime tradiderunt") what is necessary to all for salvation, and when Irenaeus writes (*Contra haereses*), "What they (the Apostles) have first preached and then according to the will of God handed on in writing, that was to be the foundation and pillar of our faith", both seem to speak of the same thing, the fact that the Scriptures contain the whole essential, necessary, gospel message. In Origen's time the unwritten tradition was already no longer marked by great clarity. M. Schmaus writes (*Katholische Dogmatik,* III, 1, p.750 ed. 1958): "In the time of the Fathers all claims to possess a new revelation going beyond that of Christ were vehemently rejected, particularly by Irenaeus, Tertullian, and Vincent of Lerin. Irenaeus of Lyons declared, against the phantasies of gnosticism, that nothing could be improved in the Apostles' propagation of the gospel. According to Irenaeus the Apostles have openly, reliably and in its entirety communicated what Christ had commanded them." Again, such words make best sense if they are applied to the gospels and other writings of the New Testament.

In his prominent work on the parables, *Die Gleichnisse Jesu* (abbreviated edition, Siebenstern-Taschenbuch, 1965 p.77) Joachim Jeremias suggests, rather convincingly, that Jesus' parables and similes contain his whole teaching: "Jesus evidently never tired of expressing the central ideas of his message in ever new similes. The parables and similes fall easily into ten groups. As a whole these comprise a complete summary of Christ's message."

Properly considered, infallibility is only a quality of knowing; it cannot be a source of knowledge about what Christ has revealed; it cannot substitute for a channel of knowledge about the contents of his revelation. For these contents the Church depends on reliable records or sources available. Only these can give her certainty – or infallible certainty. When the records are silent, or speak with an uncertain voice, where will she find the evidence that can make her "infallibly" certain that a proposition was really revealed by Christ?

Knowledge is only real knowledge when it is certain. If infallibility gives certainty of interpretation or knowledge – whilst without it we could not be certain – then it actually gives us knowledge that without it we would not have. Hence, against the traditional claim made for infallibility that it is not a source of knowledge about what Jesus revealed, it is implicitly made into a source of knowledge after all. This is borne out when applied to particular doctrines. Without infallibility we can have no certainty, and therefore no real knowledge, of the immaculate conception of Mary or her assumption with body and soul into heaven. In themselves the proofs for the revelation of these doctrines are not convincing, as theologians admit. It is therefore actually only infallibility which gives us certainty and therefore real knowledge about them. It is thus made into a source of knowledge in substitution for other evidence.

The Church's claim to infallibility, if it can be proved at all, must be proved by means of the New Testament records and very earliest tradition. (Since the earliest tradition in this matter is only a vague reflection of New Testament teaching, we need not pay attention to it.) As far as evidence goes, the New Testament books are almost the only source of certain knowledge about Christ and his revelation. If there is an infallible teaching authority in the Church, it must be demonstrated by evidence from these books. It is not infallibility which can give certainty to these books, it is they that must give us certainty about infallibility. They are the foundation on which our knowledge of the fact and major contents of the revelation and infallibility is built. If the New Testament records are unreliable, or unable to give us certain knowledge, the doctrine of infallibility must also remain uncertain. Far from adding certainty to the records, its own certainty depends entirely on these records.

Infallibility is, moreover, only one of the propositions we are confronted with in the bible. Many, if not all, major facts of Christ's life and teaching are contained more clearly in the New Testament bible than infallibility. By that very fact they are more certain than infallibility and cannot gain their certainty from it. At most, it could communicate its own degree of certainty to propositions less clearly contained in the bible than infallibility itself. It cannot give added certainty to those truths which are expressed more clearly in the bible than itself. It is, therefore, false to say that without infallibility we would have no firm foundation of faith, no means of knowing with certainty what the gospel contains, since all or most of the major facts and teachings are more certain than infallibility.

For the same reason it cannot serve as a better foundation to faith than the biblical records themselves; it is a weaker foundation. It cannot be stronger than the foundation on which it rests: that foundation is the historical reliability of the authentic biblical records. Insofar as the act of faith requires a prior certainty about the fact of revelation and its major or essential contents, this certainty is not provided by infallibility but by the records themselves and their demonstrable historical trustworthiness. To be sure, the fact that the whole Church and all its scholars agree on understanding the records in the same way strongly adds to the presumption that their understanding of them is right. A consensus adds enormously to *a priori* verisimilitude. But the presumption that they are right on the doctrine of infallibility is not as great as the presumption that they are right on other facts even more clearly contained in the records. Nor is there any consensus about the doctrine of infallibility being contained in the records, except within the Catholic Church. The consensus on other major points spreads beyond the Catholic Church and its scholars to all the other major Christian churches.

We cannot avoid basing our certainty of the fact of revelation and its major contents on a human judgement; even the doctrine of infallibility cannot be known except by a human judgement on what the records contain about it. Even if the records prove that the Church is infallible, the proof itself gives us no more than ordinary, not "infallible", certainty. It is, therefore, a vain attempt to use the doctrine of infallibility as a means to give us an infallible certainty about the fact of revelation and its contents. To make our certainty about the revelation, and our primary act of faith, depend on infallibility ties us up in a vicious circle. It is evident therefore that the primary, truly fundamental, problem is not infallibility but the trustworthiness of the New Testament books. Ultimately our certainty can only be an ordinary, not an infallible, one.

Against this the following objection has been raised. "If on the grounds of Scripture and tradition I accept the doctrine of infallibility as morally certain (let's say 90% certainty), then a doctrine that boasted only 40% certainty from other sources, if backed by the Church's infallibility should jump not just to 90% certainty (this would be according to the above argumentation) but to 100% certainty, since infallibility came in. In other words, I can accept or reject infallibility on its own merits, but if I happen to accept infallibility, even though I achieve only moral certainty, I am not free to reject doctrines proposed by the infallible magisterium, since this is just the meaning of infallibility"...Here an attempt is made to achieve 100% certainty on the basis of a proposition which is only 90% certain. This is sheer sophistry. It is similar to the attempt to make acts of faith absolutely certain by relying on God's truthfulness, when the fact of revelation is in fact only morally certain. In the total act of assent we cannot, as rational beings, abstract from the knowledge that for us the fact of revelation, or of infallibility, is only 90% certain. In the case of the act of faith we can say that we can never withdraw our act of assent because God let us down, since he never lets us down; but we can be let down, and often are, by mistaking non-revealed propositions for revealed. In the same way if propositions proposed as infallible prove to be wrong, we must either conclude that we were mistaken about the existence of infallibility or that we were under the wrong impression that infallibility was involved in the doctrines proposed. The latter is in fact what theologians have started asserting on a grand scale, as we have already noted. But we cannot make a chain stronger than its weakest link.

From the foregoing it is clear that not infallibility but ordinary certainty is the basis of our faith, at least as far as the necessary knowledge of the fact of revelation and most or all its essential parts is concerned. We have mistaken the need of certainty for the need of infallibility. Actually we are certain without it, and infallibility itself is less certain than the fact and major components of the revelation.

Inadvertently the need and role of infallibility have been much exaggerated in the Catholic scheme of things. As mentioned already, even if we ascribe infallibility to the ecclesiastical magisterium, this infallibility does not reach all the way down to the individual believer. His participation in an infallible knowledge of the Church can only be a fallible one. Experience shows how fallible. The ordinary teaching that reaches the individual Catholic is teaching exercised by parents, priests, catechists, others. None of this is infallible, though most of it will be in conformity with the official teaching of the Church. It does not save Catholics from error. Each has his very limited knowledge and large dose of misconceptions. Infallibility does not prevent this infinite variety in the mixture of error and truth. Only a few scholars know the "theological note" of what is taught in the catechisms and from the pulpits; they know what is proposed by the Church's magisterium as infallible doctrine and what degree of certainty or doubt is attached to the rest. Most Catholics are under the impression that it is all infallibly true. The Church's infallibility therefore does not take away the fallibility of the teachers and the taught. Nor can this defect be eliminated by saying that it is Christ himself or the Holy Spirit who speaks through the Church. She herself teaches that the Spirit's assistance is a negative one which prevents her from teaching as revealed and certain what in fact is not revealed or true. There is no question of her being in a positive way God's voice. But even if she were in her infallible utterances God's voice, these do not reach the individual Catholic through infallible channels. His act of faith cannot therefore be based on an infallible knowledge of what God has revealed.

After these general comments on infallibility and the bible which show that we are not dependent on infallibility for an assured knowledge of the fact and main components of Christ's revelation, nor would benefit by it so much as commonly claimed, I will try to give an analysis of the biblical testimony on which the case for it is traditionally based.

VI

THE BIBLICAL EVIDENCE FOR INFALLIBILITY

The biblical texts to which appeal is made to prove the existence of an infallible teaching authority may with some overlapping be divided into two groups. The first comprises texts that in various ways express the commission to teach entrusted to Christ's disciples and the certainty of their message or preaching; the second indicates or implies the basis of that certainty. It will suffice to point out the main texts. *We use them here as they are used in the traditional argument,* without entering into the question whether some of the words are to be really ascribed to Christ himself or rather express how the writer or early Church interpreted his mind. Only after quoting the texts will an assessment be made of their value in relation to our problem.

At the end of his stay on earth Christ gave to his disciples the solemn commission to teach. According to Matthew he said: "All authority in heaven and on earth has been given to me. Go therefore and make disciples of all nations. . . .teaching them to observe all that I have commanded you; and lo, I am with you always, to the close of the age" Mt. 28, 18-20 (compare also Mk. 16, 15-18; Lk. 24, 47-49; Acts 1,8).

Their mission is a continuation of Christ's own mission; "Jesus said to them again: 'Peace be with you.' As the Father has sent me, even so I send you." Jn. 20,21 (Jn.17,18). Christ identified himself with his disciples: "Truly, truly, I say to you, he who receives any one whom I send receives me; and he who receives me receives him who sent me" Jn. 13,20 (Mt. 10,40; Lk.10,16). Thus St. Paul can assert that Christ speaks in him (2 Cor. 13,3), and that his teaching is not the word of man, but of God (1 Thes. 2, 13; Gal. 1, 11-12).

The Apostles are convinced of this mission and act with confidence as teachers of the truth (Acts 2,14-40.42; 3,11-26); Paul appeals to this commision (Acts. 22,21).

The certainty of their teaching is proved by the fact that Christ remains with them in their teaching (Mt. 28,20), that the Holy Spirit will bring all things to their mind and lead them into all truth (Jn. 14,26; 16,13), and by the words reported in Mark: "He who believes and is baptized shall be saved; but be who does not believe will be condemned," Mk. 16,16. Miracles confirmed their preaching (Mk. 16,20).

St. Paul writes, Gal. 1, 8-9: "Even if we, or an angel from heaven, should preach to you a gospel contrary to that which we preached to you, let him be accursed. As we have said before, so now I say again, if any one is preaching to you a gospel contrary to that which you received, let him be accursed." He also speaks of God "inflicting vengeance... upon those who do not obey the gospel" 2 Thes. 1,8. St. John warns not to receive into the house or give a greeting to anyone who does not bring this doctrine of Christ (2 Jn. 10-11). In 1 Tim. 3,15 St. Paul calls the church "the pillar and bulwark of the truth."

The second group of texts indicates or suggests the reason for the certainty the Apostles and disciples have of their teaching. Two different reasons are mentioned. The larger number bases the certainty on the fact that they are witnesses, eye - and earwitnesses, of what they preach, or that their testimony is based on such first-hand witness. A smaller number speaks of Christ or the Holy Spirit being with them or guiding them.

John mentions the first-rate character of his testimony several times. In Jn. 19,35 he writes: "He who saw it has borne witness – his witness is true, and he knows that he tells the truth – that you also may believe." Again at the end of his gospel, Jn. 21,24: "This is the disciple who is bearing witness to these things, and who has written these things; and we know that his testimony is true". To show that he remembers many more things, he adds in the next verse with much exaggeration: "But there are many other things which Jesus did; were every one of them to be written, I suppose that the world itself could not contain the books that would be written." Already at the beginning of his gospel, Jn. 1,14, he wrote of his personal knowledge: "And the Word became flesh and dwelt among us, full of grace and truth; we have beheld his glory, glory as of the only Son from the Father." His strongest appeal to the first-class nature of his testimony is found in his first letter, 1 Jn. 1,1-5: "That which was from the beginning, which we have heard, which we have seen with our eyes, which we have looked upon and touched with our hands, concerning the word of life – the life was made manifest, and we saw it, and testify to it, and proclaim to you the eternal life which was with the Father and was made manifest to us – that which we have seen and heard we proclaim also to you, so that you may have fellowship with us; and our fellowship is with the Father and with his Son Jesus Christ. And we are writing this that our (your) joy may be complete. This is the message we have heard from him and proclaim to you..".

Luke too is emphatic in basing his writings on first-hand witness. In the prologue to his gospel he writes of the trouble he has taken to make sure that he will give a reliable account: "Inasmuch as many have undertaken to compile a narrative of the things which have been accomplished among us, just as they were delivered to us by those who from the beginning were eyewitnesses and ministers of the word, it seemed good to me also, having followed all things closely for some time past, to write an orderly account for you, most excellent Theophilus, that you may know the truth concerning the things of which you have been informed", Lk. 1,1-4. The Apostles were to be witnesses of Christ and his message. Thus at the end of Luke's gospel, Christ is said to have told them what to preach to all nations and added, "You are witnesses of these things", Lk. 24,48. The same in Acts 1,8: "You shall receive power when the Holy Spirit has come upon you; and you shall be my witnesses in Jerusalem and in all Judea and Samaria and to the end of the earth" (see also Acts 1,22; 10,39; 20,24). Paul appeals to many witnesses to prove the truth of Christ's resurrection, 1 Cor. 15, 3-8, and speaks of witnessing elsewhere, 1 Cor. 11,23; Gal. 1, 11-12. In Gal. 2, 1-2 he mentions that he went to Jerusalem to lay his gospel before the leading Apostles "Lest somehow I should be running or had run in vain". This does not sound like a man relying on or appealing to his "infallibility", but like one relying on trustworthy witnesses. Also Peter speaks of his having been a witness of Christ's majesty, 2 Pet. 1,16.

The other reason for certainty lies in the fact that Christ will be with the Apostles, as mentioned in Mt. 28,20, and promised to send them the Holy Spirit who "will teach you all things, and bring to your remembrance all that I have said to you", Jn. 14,26; and "will guide you into all the truth" Jn. 16,13 (Jn. 14,16-17; 15,26-27; 16,7-15). In Acts 1,8 we already saw that Christ connects their witnessing with the coming of the Spirit; in Acts 5,32 Peter and other Apostles answered to the Jewish Council: "We are witnesses to these things, and so is the Holy Spirit whom God has given to those who obey him." Another appeal to the Holy Spirit is found in the decision taken by the council of Jerusalem: "It has seemed good to the Holy Spirit and to us..." Acts 15,28.

For the purpose of this thesis which deals with the claim to infallibility as actually made by the Church, it is not permissible to restrict the object of infallibility to the central core of the gospel message. Though the arguments proposed apply also to such a reduced object, this paper deals with infallibility as taught by the magisterium, which extends to a large number of doctrines or dogmas that can be considered in partial isolation.

In the traditional argument for infallibility great weight is given to the first group of texts which prove that Christ gave to his disciples the commission to teach all he had commanded them, and that their teaching is so certain that those who wilfully disbelieve will be condemned. On closer consideration, however, it becomes obvious that these texts do not prove or imply infallibility. What they say is only that Christ wanted them to teach his gospel and that they have certain knowledge of what to teach. This tells us nothing of the manner in which they would have sufficient and certain knowledge.

We have already seen the need of a body of teachers. Christ's gospel is meant for all men, as a message of salvation and joy. A great majority of people can only be reached and convinced by oral preaching. Even when books are available, the work cannot be delegated to the printed pages, because many people are either illiterate or otherwise unqualified or unwilling to study Christ's message for themselves. In its own secular field society knows of no other means than oral teaching to impart to its members the initial knowledge needed for present-day tasks and living.

To be able to teach, the men appointed by Christ must have the necessary knowledge. This knowledge must be reliable or certain, based on sufficient evidence. In the case of the Apostles, Christ himself had trained them and kept them with him to witness his words and deeds. His personality and message and his miraculous works – to which he himself appealed as proof – demonstrated to them that he was speaking as one sent by God and that his message was true.

When the Apostles were sent out to preach, they were well prepared. Individually and as a group they had such unforgettable memories of all the main events and teachings of Jesus that they could not err in communicating them to their audiences. There was no need in their case of a special charism of inerrancy. Their infallibility was not of the theological but of the natural kind which is another name for unshakably certain knowledge. For a long period of time they had personally heard and seen Jesus. They had often reminisced about him and discussed among themselves the meaning of it all. Christ's death and resurrection and the descent of the Spirit on Pentecost placed his person and teaching for them into final perspective and thus completed their initiation into their task.

When after Pentecost they set out to preach, they appealed to what they had heard and seen and to events of which many hundreds and thousands had been witnesses. Occasionally they could also appeal to miracles and to the miraculous manifestations of "the Holy Spirit whom God has given to those who obey him", Acts 5,32. But these extraordinary happenings seem to have been a passing phase needed for a faster initial break-through. Their common appeal was to their personal knowledge,the testimony of eye - and earwitnesses, which was confirmed by their whole life and devotion and readiness to suffer all hardships in the service of Christ. When preaching to non-believers their appeal could only be to this natural source of certain knowledge. An appeal to a personal prerogative of infallibility or to a special invisible assistance of the Holy Spirit, neither of them subject to proof, would have been invalid, and ineffective, at least with intelligent and common-sense listeners. Such an appeal was therefore never made by them. When they speak of the Holy Spirit, it is to mention the fact of his assistance, never directly to appeal to it as proof that their teaching is true.

The words of Mark 16,16 that those who will not believe will be condemned, and of Paul, Gal. 1, 8-9, "Even if we, or an angel from heaven, should preach to you a gospel contrary to that which we preached to you, let him be accursed...", express in particularly strong terms both the certainty of the gospel message as well as the moral obligation for the hearer to accept it.

But even these words imply only certainty, not a charism of infallibility. The Apostles were so certain of the major events of Jesus' life and his message that nothing could shake their conviction. On what was it based? On a prerogative of infallibility? or only on their sure memory of what they had heard and seen? They themselves appeal regularly to the latter reason. All of us have similar certainties which no contradiction can shake. Not only of very recent happenings, as that we ate breakfast this morning or met friends yesterday, but also of events further in the past. Bishops who took part in the second Vatican Council are so sure of having met that they can say: Even if an angel from heaven told otherwise, he would be wrong.

As for the obligation incurred by those who hear the message and the consequences if they refuse to accept it, even the Church does not deny that the threat is only directed at those hearers who refuse to believe in spite of recognizing its truth. And how are they to recognize it? By perceiving (on what evidence?) that the preachers have the prerogative of infallibility? Or by inferring that they can be sure that the preachers are honest men and know what they speak about? Christ does not say that they will be condemned even if, in spite of good will, they do not detect the validity of the claims made for the message. His words do not prescind from proof or evidence, on the contrary they imply that these are available. They do not indicate a preaching based on infallibility, but one based on evidence good enough to provide reasonable certainty to the listener of good will that what the preachers say is true.

There are other reasons for rejecting the inference from the existence of a moral obligation to the existence of a charism of infallibility. All other grave obligations are based on ordinary, not infallible, certainties, as those imposed by natural law or lawful authority. It is enough that the obligation is morally certain for us to be bound by it. Why should the obligation in this case demand infallible certainty? Moreover, as noted already, the knowledge about the existence of infallibility, if any, does not precede, it follows that of the revelation. Only after we already know that Christ is a true messenger from God, does the question arise of the Church and its competence, including infallibility. The knowledge of the revelation and the corresponding obligation to accept it precede any possible knowledge of infallibility and are therefore not based on infallibility but only on ordinary certainty.

The mission given to the Apostles has a parallel in the sending out, two by two, of the seventy disciples as narrated by Luke 10, 1-20, (cf also Mt.10). Those who refuse to listen to them are threatened by Jesus, "I tell you, it shall be more tolerable on that day for Sodom than for that town." He also tells the disciples, "He who hears you hears me, and he who rejects you rejects me...". We have here exactly the kind of mission later given to the Apostles, with the same assurance that they speak in Jesus' name, and the same threat to those who will not listen. Yet, no one would claim that in this particular preaching assignment the seventy had a charism of infallibility bestowed on them.

The Apostles and other disciples could appeal to their personal knowledge as proof of the truth of what they preached. They were speaking in the strict sense of the word as witnesses. Because of the circumstances in which their testimony was told, or written down, and accepted, their testimony established its own trustworthiness. For their audiences this obvious trustworthiness was its evidence of truth.

What of the other preachers in their time and of those coming after them? They cannot appeal to personal knowledge; they have to appeal therefore to the knowledge or testimony of the original witnesses. For them, as for other listeners, both the knowledge contained in the testimony and the evidence of its truth are to be found in the Apostles' witness. In its oral form this witness has gone with the wind * but in its written form it has been preserved in the many writings of the New Testament. This means that the

*Not without leaving its results in the establishment and spread of the Church; but we have no demonstrable access to the oral preaching except insofar as it is preserved in its written reflection in the New Testament books.

very testimony of the Apostles – its contents and its evidence – which convinced their contemporaries and led to the rapid spread of the gospel, is still with us, in authentic written accounts.

It would seem evident, therefore, that later preachers are dependent on this written testimony for their certain knowledge. It is not enough that they have been appointed as official preachers. To be able to carry out their task, they must have access to the necessary knowledge and evidence. Besides, if the listeners are obliged to accept their preaching, under the threat of condemnation, they too, or at least the educated and intelligent among them, those who demand evidence and can verify the preaching also for others, must have access to the same evidence and knowledge. For both, therefore, preachers and audience, the final fount of the gospel message is in the New Testament books, the only extant documents connecting us with verifiable certainty with Jesus and his message.

To approach the problem from another angle. Either the knowledge and evidence are still available, or not. If still available, they will be accessible both to the teachers and to those listeners who are of equal good will and intelligence and take the same trouble to study them. If they are no longer available, both teachers and listeners can have no access to them. But how, in that case, can the teachers know with certainty what to teach and how can the listeners be obliged, on penalty of damnation, to accept their teaching?

To this last question the reply given by the Church is: Christ entrusted his revealed truth to the living magisterium. Under the guidance of the Holy Spirit this can know with infallible certainty even revealed truth for which no convincing evidence is found in the New Testament books or in a demonstrably uninterrupted historical tradition. The infallible magisterium is not dependent for certainty on outside, independent, evidence. Its infallible decisions have the real ground of their certainty in themselves, or, ultimately, in the assistance of the Holy Spirit.

From what we have seen till now, the first group of biblical texts – about the commission to teach and the certainty of the teaching – do not prove or suggest infallibility. And even what seems to us a strong suggestion would not be good enough. Tradition, education, mental conditioning, play a trick on us. It makes it possible for whole societies to accept as quite probable, as not at all difficult to believe, as "demonstrated" on only the flimsiest grounds, propositions which to the non-conditioned person appear utterly unlikely or fantastic. Well-known instances are the belief of traditional societies in mythological stories and in astrology. There is need of especially sound evidence to prove what is in itself most improbable.

Most texts of the second group show that the Apostles and their disciples appeal to personal knowledge or testimony. They base their teaching not on a prerogative of infallibility or a special assistance of the Holy Spirit, but on ordinary first-hand knowledge. This same first-hand knowledge or witness, preserved in its written form in the New Testament books, seems to supply the necessary knowledge and evidence also to later preachers. Anyway, it is the only recognizable and demonstrable major and first-rate source of knowledge we have of Jesus' life and teaching.

The biblical case for infallibility must therefore rest on Christ's promise to remain with his disciples and on those texts which speak of the assistance of the Holy Spirit.

It is perhaps illicit to extend the promise of the Holy Spirit's assistance, made to the Apostles, to their successors. His role is described as bringing to remembrance all that Jesus had said to them. That he will teach them all truth, seems to refer to the same thing. The obvious meaning of "remembrance" makes the words applicable only to the Apostles, and the same is suggested by the words "all that I have said to you".

It has become a generally accepted doctrine in the Church that revelation was not concluded with Christ, but went on till the death of the last Apostle. Probably this idea was suggested by Christ's words on the role of the Holy Spirit and by belief in the inspiration of the New Testament books. But is it valid? The Apostles themselves speak only of witnessing to what Christ himself had said and done; they never suggest that they were given any revelation adding to his. If the words about the Holy Spirit do really imply further revelations, and if they are also applicable to the successors of the Apostles, it is not apparent why they should not apply to these successors in their full meaning.

However, Christ's command to teach all nations, as reported by Matthew and Mark, certainly implies that he, and therefore the Spirit, will be also with the successors of the Apostles. The same seems implied in Jesus' words to the Apostles, as reported by John 14,16, that the Father "will give you another Counsellor, to be with you for ever, even the Spirit of truth." Concerning the Apostles themselves, Christians believe in the supernatural origin of the revelation given them by Christ, as well as in their special enlightenment by the Spirit on Pentecost and perhaps occasionally afterwards. It seems, however, natural to suppose that in trying to remember the main events and teachings of Jesus that formed the substance of the gospel, and in trying to understand their implications in the light of later developments, the Apostles were able to do so without a special divine assistance.

With regard to Jesus' promise, therefore, that he and the Spirit will remain with the disciples and their successors, the question arises: Does he speak of a special divine assistance which might perhaps allow us to admit a prerogative of infallibility, or does he speak only of ordinary, though effective, providential divine assistance? Or, in other words, how does the Spirit operate in the Church and enable Jesus' disciples and their successors to teach all revealed truth? Is it by a charism of infallibility, or is it by inspiring them with a faithful love of Jesus and his gospel that will prompt them in fulfilment of their task, to write down his gospel in good time and later to remain for ever faithful to this written testimony? If theologians make much of the Spirit's inner testimony, what else does this amount to than this faithful love by which he opens the believers' minds for an understanding of the gospel and makes them ready to interpret it in faithful fellowship with the other members of the Christian community?

It is an accepted principle of exegesis, as it is of common sense, that we are not allowed to accept an extraordinary or supernatural explanation when an ordinary, natural one is possible. Moreover, the ordinary way in which God achieves his purposes is by endowing his creatures with all the qualities, means, and tendencies required to lead to the end intended by him. In this way even the marvel of evolution, from inorganic matter to man, seems to have taken place.

The question therefore is: Has Christ done everything to leave further developments to his Church or disciples?

There is first the question of certainty, of trustworthy testimony accessible through the ages. We have this in the New Testament books. The Church must appeal to it in trying to win an unbelieving world over to Christ. Infallibility can add nothing to its certainty. It is not self-evident, and depends itself on that same testimony.

To this must be added the overwhelmingly attractive and imposing personality of Christ; the importance of his message in solving man's major existential problems; the love, trust and fidelity which his personality and message cannot fail to awaken in many listeners to the gospel; the gathering of these into one Church; and the commission given to them to preach his gospel to all nations. Who can say that these factors are not sufficient to guarantee the preservation and passing on of the whole substance of his gospel? With a fraction of these advantages Islam has managed to preserve its message for more than thirteen centuries, whilst Buddhism, Hinduism, Jainism, and other religions have survived fairly intact in their major ideas for a much longer time than Christianity. If we think of the future, the prospects of Christianity seem to be even brighter. Mankind becomes ever more rational and scientific. Its leading exponents demand evidence and are willing to submit to it. What can be proved is assured of a future. Need we doubt that in God's ordinary providence all these factors guarantee the preservation and spread of the Church and the gospel?

This does not mean of course that Christianity does not need a natural preparedness in those it approaches in order to win them over to Christ. In its final stage this preparedness may be called an open mind, good will, readiness to give evidence its full weight, but meanwhile a long development may be required to reach this final stage of preparation. As on the social and cultural so on the religious plane, a high level of prior achievement is often the most formidable obstacle to further advance. Whilst primitive peoples, for example, make an easy leap from illiteracy to the simple efficiency of the Roman script, China continues to labour under the frightful burden, but astounding cultural achievement, of a script with more than 40,000 signs.

In *Die Gleichnisse Jesu* (Siebenstern-Taschenbuch, 1965, p.144) Jeremias explains that with his comparison of the city set on a hill Jesus wished to brace his disciples and save them from discouragement. They will be like a city on the hill that will withstand all onslaughts of its enemies and whose light will shine far into the night without need of human effort. Having the gospel, they have all they need for their work. If they have faith, even if no bigger than a mustard seed, nothing will be impossible to them. This seems to confirm that with the gospel Christ has provided all the means needed to make his work succeed even without further special divine intervention.

Leaving out reports of miracles said to have happened after the Apostolic era, we may well ask: Is there anything in the history of the Church that cannot be explained by natural causes, without special divine guidance? Do not the many failures, the schisms and their causes, the vice and folly in all ranks, rather indicate that God has entrusted his work fully into human hands and laid on us the responsibility for its successes and failures? We still think too much in categories of a by-gone age; in the history of the Church we must shed the myth (as we have already shed it in other fields) that God continuously enters into the chain of secondary causes.

There is another reason why the texts on the Holy Spirit cannot be taken as evidence for a special or extraordinary assistance, as is supposed by the doctrine of infallibility. Christ spoke to people whose knowledge of natural causes was very limited, who saw everywhere a direct working of God. For them the boundaries between ordinary and extra-ordinary divine providence were wrongly drawn. It was necessary for them to know that Christ's work would not fall, that it had a great future. As for how it would prosper they depended for understanding on their own primitive view of the world. It would have been impossible to explain it to them in any other terms. For us who know better, there is no reason why we should interpret the encouraging words of Jesus as a promise of extraordinary assistance.

Suppose that in an instruction on divine providence Jesus had spoken to his disciples about the gradual development of higher forms of life from lower ones. Because of current primitive views he could not have explained it in terms of the modern theory of evolution; this would have made no sense to them. He would have simply told them that God directed the process. This would have fitted in with his intention, which was to teach religion, not natural science. The same applies to the commission to teach all nations. He could only speak in terms of God-the-Spirit—guiding and helping his disciples in their apparently impossible task. Only such a view suited their general understanding of things, to which Jesus had to accommodate himself. This does not mean that Jesus shared their primitive way of understanding God's work or that we are still obliged to understand it in the way the disciples did.

Matthew tells us that Jesus warned his Apostles that they would be dragged before councils, governors, and kings, but comforted them with the promise: "When they deliver you up, do not be anxious how you are to speak or what you are to say; for what you are to say will be given you in that hour; for it is not you who speak, but the Spirit of your Father speaking through you" Mt. 10,19-20 (Lk. 12,12). Taken literally these words indicate even more definitely than the other promises that the Spirit himself will direct the minds and speech of the Apostles. Yet it seems evident that they are not to be taken literally, that they are only a promise that (by their love and knowledge) they will be stimulated to the right words for the occasion.

There is another major objection to the attempt to use the Joannine texts about the Spirit of Truth (Jn. 14,16-17. 26; 15, 26-27; 16,7-15) as proof for a charism of infallibility. In the total context it is not at all clear what the exact meaning is of those words attributed to Jesus.

In introducing the promise of the Spirit of Truth for the first time, Jesus makes his mission dependent on the disciples' love: "If you love me, you will keep my commandments. And I will pray the Father, and he will give you another Counsellor, to be with you for ever, even the Spirit of Truth whom the world cannot receive, because it neither sees him nor knows him; you know him, for he dwells with you, and will be in you," Jn.14, 15-17. An assistance by the Spirit which is dependent on a love great enough to keep the commandments does not seem the kind with which infallibility is concerned. This operates independently from such love; all popes and general councils are infallible that intentionally pronounce solemn definitions. John reports mysterious words. Shortly before, in verses 12-14, Jesus is quoted as having said: "Truly, truly, I say to you, he who believes in me will also do the works that I do; and greater works than these will he do, because I go to the Father. Whatever you ask in my name, I will do it, that the Father may be glorified in the Son; if you ask anything in my name, I will do it." How can we make these words literally true that the believers in him will do even greater works than Jesus did and that they receive all they ask for?* Yet it is in this same context that he speaks of the Spirit who will lead them into all truth and bring all things to their remembrance. Can we be sure that we can take these words at maximum face value, that they can even be used as evidence for a charism of infallibility? Or must we be satisfied with knowing that those who love Jesus will understand truly and fully what he wished to reveal, without our being able to pinpoint what this really implies: does he mean the depth of God's love (what St. Paul called the mystery hidden from the beginning of the world) and the major facts from which this love is known, or does he imply (also) a complete list of propositions that might be culled from what Jesus said in his instructions to his disciples?

Later in the same discourse he seems to refer only to the essential understanding of the Father and the Son: "This is eternal life, that they know thee the only true God, and Jesus Christ whom thou hast sent" Jn. 17,3; "I have given them the words which thou gavest me, and they have received them and know in truth that I came from thee; and they have believed that thou didst send me", Jn. 17,8 (Jn. 17,6-8. 17-26). In the context of this discourse it seems impossible to use the words about the Spirit of Truth as evidence for a prerogative of infallibility as understood and exercised by the Church in more recent times.

The readiness with which masses of Jews and Gentiles were admitted into the Christian community after a single instruction – 3000 on Pentecost day (Acts 2,41); many more after the cure of a lame beggar (Acts 4,4); and ever new members in larger or smaller groups – shows that it was not belief in a detailed array of truths, but a new outlook on life and faith in God as manifested by Jesus (and as readily

*To meet the difficulties arising from contrary experience St. Augustine argued that these latter words apply only to whatever is conducive to the salvation of the person praying. If we now believe that God intervenes directly in the ordinary course of events only very rarely, we must define Jesus' promise still further. All that man really desires and therefore prays for is an abiding fulfilling love and happiness. In full measure this is bestowed on us only in heaven, though already now we can share in it. Jesus promises present sharing and future fulfilment to all who remain in intimate union with their heavenly Father by constant prayer.

understood by unsophisticated people, whilst often "hidden" to the tradition-bound and wordly wise, Mt. 11,25-27, Lk. 10,21-22) that made the converts Christians and members of the Church. Though it is in the nature of the educated mind to search for all the possible implications or ramifications of what Jesus revealed, it seems highly improbable that he commissioned or intended to enable his disciples to impose their acceptance as an indispensable condition of Church membership.

Once we accept that Christ is God, we must believe that the whole substance of his gospel will in fact be preserved throughout the ages, as intended by him. The question is only: What does that substance comprise and how is its preservation achieved?

Christ's religion is identical with the total reality of his gospel, and its preservation guaranteed by its continued existence among men. The gospel has found a twofold, permanent, visible expression: in the written apostolic testimony and in the Church or community of Christ's disciples. It is through the interaction of these two that the whole substance of the gospel is preserved and remains a living reality. It is not dissimilar to what happened in the people of ancient Israel. All the major insights about God and his providence were preserved and continued to grow from generation to generation, without any prerogative of infallibility in those who were its official teachers. Jesus himself acknowledged: "The scribes and the Pharisees sit on Moses' seat; so practise and observe what they tell you..." Mt. 23,2; and of the scribes he declared that they possessed "the key of knowledge" (Lk. 11,52). Though these words strongly remind us of the role later assigned to the ecclesiastical magisterium, they have never been understood to imply that the scribes and Pharisees had a charism of infallibility.

If the community of believers had no authentic testimony to be guided by, the original revelation could hardly be kept from gradual dissolution without a special divine guidance. But this is not the situation at all. On the contrary, the community has at its disposal in a permanent form the original testimony of the Apostles themselves. Why should we be able to know with certainty what Plato taught and not what Jesus taught?

We must not make too much of the apparently contrary experience of the Protestants. The Reformation was a battle against abuses and against particular teachings of the Church which were not obviously contained in the bible. In the bitterness of its reaction its pendulum swung too far in the other direction. Most churches of the Reformation have given up the individualistic principle of interpretation of the bible long ago; in fact many recognized its insufficiency from the beginning. The new French Ecumenical Bible states categorically that "the Churches of the Reformation have constantly affirmed that they recognize, as sovereign and final authority in matters of faith, holy scripture read in the communion of the Church and in conformity with the ecumenical creeds."

Facts do not bear out that infallibility has been the main guarantee of unity among Christ's followers and of the preservation of the substance of the gospel. This very infallibility, with its many doctrinal claims that go beyond the clear teachings of the gospels, is actually a major cause of disunity among Christians and forced Church authorities in the past to expel many millions of believing Christians who had honest differences of opinion that would otherwise have been discussed, and resolved, within the Church itself. The fact that after the schism the Orthodox churches have preserved without infallibility the essentials of the gospel for a thousand years and that the trinitarian and christological dogmas have survived until today among Protestants who believe in a divine revelation, shows that it is not infallibility that is responsible for the preservation of the substance of the gospel, but precisely faithfulness to Christ as portrayed in the authentic gospel accounts. It is true that being more tolerant of dissent Protestant churches retained within their communities many who lost faith in the supernatural contents of the scriptures; this must not make us lose sight of the fact that, in spite of infallibility and excommunication, the Catholic Church lost in advanced countries perhaps an equal percentage of her members to unbelief.

To approach the same problem from a somewhat different angle. Admittedly there must be a possibility of certainty about the essentials of the gospel and thus a foundation of possible unity. One of the conditions is of a subjective nature. There can be no certainty and unity of faith without good will and faithfullness to the apostolic testimony, nor without sufficient readiness to submit one's private opinion to the final judgement of the community. These are common-sense conditions, but only where there is love of Christ can they be fulfilled.

If we look for an objective basis of certainty about Jesus and his mission we depend on reliable historical records. Before we can begin to think of infallibility as a foundation of truth and unity, we have to find a more basic one on which infallibility itself depends. Infallibility can be considered only after we have already become certain of Jesus' divine mission. This preceding certainty is of a historical nature and is based almost entirely on the New Testament books originating and embedded in the oral preaching or tradition of the time of the Apostles. It is this historical certainty which is the preamble of Christian faith that makes it possible for the Christian community to believe in Christ.

But certainty is required about all the essentials of the gospel. Do the records provide the same historical certainty, which they give for Jesus' mission, for all the fundamentals of the gospel? Do they contain with sufficient clarity its whole substance? If so, the possibility of certainty and unity is assured even without infallibility: we can have the same historical certainty about all the essentials that we must be satisfied with in the case of the most basic fact of all, Jesus' divine mission. Only if we must postulate, only if it can be proved, that not all the essentials are clearly enough contained in the New Testament books, shall we have reason to make the further postulate that in addition to those records there must be another means, an infallible Church or magisterium, to enable us to know with certainty also those revealed truths which are not clearly enough contained in the apostolic records. But is such a postulate reasonable, is it what common sense leads us to expect? Is it likely that the authors of the gospel accounts who have written down hundreds of minor details, of minutiae that cannot be part of the gospel except to bring out more clearly Jesus' uniqueness, should have left out, all four of them, some truly essential parts of his role and message? *A priori* this seems most unlikely; it is only under the influence of belief in infallibility that we Catholics have become accustomed to believe that the Church has access to many revealed truths for which there is no clear evidence in the gospels. We are, in fact, faced with a choice between two suppositions: (1) The gospel accounts and other New Testament books give the Church with sufficient clarity the whole substance of Christ's revelation; (2) They fail to do so and, therefore, the Holy Spirit especially assists the Church throughout the ages to enable her to teach infallibly the whole revealed truth. The first supposition indicates what seems natural and to be expected; the second represents a view that must now be called *a priori* most improbable and due entirely to a primitive understanding of the working of God's providence.

Once we admit that all the essentials are clearly enough contained in the New Testament records, there is the possibility of certainty and unity without infallibility. Good will and faithfulness to the records and willingness to leave final judgement to the community are still required. There is also need of sufficient time, study and discussion to come to a consensus about the essentials (as we know from the example of the christological and trinitarian controversies). But there will be no need of infallibility, since an ordinary historical certainty which must do as a preamble of faith for the basic fact of Christ's mission, and for infallibility itself if it did exist, will also suffice for faith in the other essentials.

The command given to the Church to teach the gospel to all nations and the conviction she always had of being able to do so, harmonize well with the need and possibility of valid certainty; they do not prove a charism of infallibility. The need for it would only arise if she has a right to make herself independent of the only known records and can claim certainty about the revealed character of propositions not clearly contained in them.

There is in the Church genuine progress in understanding the gospel and in applying it to her own and mankind's problems. The process was started by the Apostles themselves, and by St. Paul in a big way. There seems, however, no reason to assume that this progress, beyond the original gospel, is under a safeguard of infallibility. New insights have to be tested, re-thought and revised all the time, and solutions must be found for ever new problems. The demands of life itself impose this task on the community. Sometimes study and discussion will lead to unanimity of view, but even this is no guarantee of infallibility: it only assures the best solution possible within the knowledge and opinions of that age. All the roads must be kept open for further revision and advance, since the Church, too, can only develop through trial and error. As long as she remains faithful to the original testimony, her mistakes, her imperfect solutions, do no real harm to the work of the gospel in the world; they are but a sign that the gospel can be effective only within the limits of the knowledge, and good will, of each age. They do not prevent an ever more effective penetration of the gospel into the human mass. In this context of growth belief in infallibility is an obstacle to progress and to the gospel's effectiveness; it mistakes interim solutions for permanent ones, it partly obstructs the way to new knowledge and the meeting of new problems and needs. The only divine, indispensable leaven is the gospel itself; all the rest is dough that must remain forever exposed to its working. Special divine interventions or guidance would only be needed if the gospel leaven were somehow defective, unequal to the task of gradually leavening the inert mass. But Jesus said, "The kingdom of heaven is like this. A man scatters seed on the land; he goes to bed at night and gets up in the morning, and the seed sprouts and grows – how, he does not know. The ground produces a crop by itself, first the blade, then the ear, then full-grown corn in the ear; but as soon as the crop is ripe, he sets to work with the sickle, because harvest-time has come", Mk. 4,26-29 (New English Bible). What is divine and does not fail is the original seed and its power; the later insights are human responses, man's attempts to fit the divine gospel to the knowledge and problems of the time. They are not final or infallible, only fragmentary and conditional.

In traditional Catholic teaching it is said of individual bishops that they are only "witnesses of the faith", not "judges of the faith", not qualified to decide questions which are still undecided or controverted. It seems this must be said of the entire Church, also of popes and ecumenical councils. Their task is to be witnesses of Christ's revelation which is preserved in the original authentic records. Their preaching must be based on solid knowledge or evidence: this gives them good certainty, but not "infallible" certainty in the theological sense. They have no commission or knowledge to decide controversies that have not yet led to a clear issue or to define doctrines as revealed for which evidence is lacking to prove their revealed character. They must always remain open to correction, which can go together with the conviction, founded on what the records prove, that the substance of the gospel will not be overthrown.

The *Constitution on the Church* of Vatican II, Chapter III, No.25, calls the bishops "teachers endowed with Christ's authority." But is "authority" the right word? They received the order or commission to teach. Those who are under orders are under obedience to do a thing, in this case to preach the gospel. As such they have no authority to go beyond the recognized gospel, nor a right to impose the revealed truth but only to propose it. The listeners' obligation to accept it is not motivated by the authority of the teachers but by the recognition that it is Christ's gospel they teach. Their subordination is not to the teachers but to the gospel. A commission to teach does not as such imply any authority over those who are taught, though some authority may be delegated together with it, as in the case of minors taught in schools. The commission given to the Apostles is to teach all nations; that is, all who do not yet believe; over these they have no authority; they can only propose the gospel to them. Is their task of teaching in regard to believers a different one? Does it, for example, include a right to demand "a religious obedience" to doctrines not recognizably part of the gospel? Does it carry any obligation to accept what is not recognized as revealed or true?

After having shown that the biblical evidence does not bear out the claim to infallibility, a word must be said about the advantages of having a teaching authority that knows that it is fallible. It will act with greater willingness to allow debate, to discuss, to listen to contrary evidence; not so hasty to reject and condemn; more conscious that it cannot rely on convictions extant in the Church but must be able to prove them. All this will favor an open, questioning mind and a serious study of the authentic documents and all later evidence.

One argument for infallibility is that if the Church were not infallible, it could become the victim of error... It seems we have an excessive fear of error, even of temporary errors of secondary importance. Through its faithfulness to the original records the Church is always able to correct errors that go against the substance of the gospel. Infallibility has not succeeded in saving the Church, its popes, bishops, and other members, from error and ignorance. The former literalistic interpretation of the bible was cause of a great mass of errors about the contents of the bible. As will be shown in a later chapter, quite a number of other doctrines which were generally believed to be part of the revealed deposit, had later to be abandoned or revised. Belief in infallibility made the correction only more difficult. History proves that errors are unavoidable and in most cases not nearly as fatal as they are made out to be. Many are innocuous or do only little harm. Ignorance of the solution of urgent problems does much more harm than error in problems that are not urgent, yet the Church is not spared her large dose of ignorance. She has been as impotent as others in finding a fair and effective solution for the problems that beset mankind. Ignorance and error are part of the human condition in religious matters and also in the Church. As long as controversies are not resolved, one or all of the contesting schools are in ignorance or error about the points disputed. When the questions are of a theoretical nature, not obviously affecting human needs, no one thinks of the continuation of the uncertainty as a calamity. It affords an opportunity for sharpening theological wits and often produces a number of side benefits, somewhat in the way research done on space projects pays for itself by the new knowledge and technical processes discovered. Have doctrinal decisions been uniformly healthy or important for the life of the Church? Can any one say with assurance that devotion to Mary has benefited, been made deeper, healthier, more enlightened, by the dogmatic definitions of her immaculate conception and assumption into heaven? And so it is with other dogmas not evidently contained in the bible, but later taught by councils or popes. Sometimes the attention seems to be drawn away too much from the main contents of gospel teaching towards notions of secondary importance. This seems to be what happened when indulgences were given an excessive weight, when Mary occupied too independent or large a place in popular devotion, when belief in the physical eucharistic presence drove into the background God's presence everywhere, when the grave obligation attached to commandments of the Church distorted in many the sense of sin at the expense of justice and charity, when the absolution from sins so readily obtained in confession lessened rather than heightened in many Catholics the urgency of a true inner conversion.

Reliance on an infallible teaching authority has not been such a healthy thing. It seems to have been largely responsible for the passive attitude towards the gospel message* and for an excessive timidity in tackling new problems. Instead of being a power towards progress and salutary change, the Church turned into an institution fearful of change and concerned with safeguarding its own positions.** Thus more than once she dragged her feet, and had to be forced by overwhelming evidence to change her stand, after most of the world had already gone ahead of her. And these were all positions that were not an evident part of Christ's gospel as recorded in the New Testament but positions which she had generally taught and which she could no longer admit as subject to discussion and doubt. It encouraged an attitude of passive waiting for Rome to move, for Rome to find solutions, to clear up messes, to lay down the law. It allowed the work of evangelization to bog down in a sterile attempt to introduce a foreign organization, with foreign cultural forms and laws, into ancient cultures to which the Church had the commission to bring the incomparable riches of Christ, not the doubtful blessings of a foreign mould. And because of her claim to infallibility even

In his *We Are All Brothers* (Herder & Herder, N.Y.) Louis Evely makes the damning observation which many a priest till a few years ago could confirm, "Every time that I have been asked an interesting question regarding religion, it has come from a non-believer. Catholics have no questions to ask. They feel certain that they know all about it... Whenever I see a copy of the Gospel in someone's hand, I know at once that he is either a recent convert or an unbeliever. Catholics are inoculated."

****Of old, priests in Egypt, India, and elsewhere, made a monopoly of their learning, and of the power that went with it, conducting it into channels controlled by them. Has the ecclesiastical magisterium perhaps, unconsciously, fallen victim to an old temptation?**

In his book *Geloof en Wereld* (Patmos, 1961,p.22-23) A. Dondeyne points out that with regard to the three great events which have moulded the modern world, namely modern science, the rise of democratic liberties, and the social breakthrough, the Church has been "very slow, hesitant, and fearful, turned more towards the past than towards the future."

The Church's opposition to change and intellectual liberty was, it seems, also the main cause for the development in Latin countries of a powerful freemasonry that was bitterly hostile to the Church.

her good arguments cease to be effective. Behind them outsiders suspect specious pleadings, not honest attempts to find the truth. Because of it the teaching Church has become like a dead thing that must be moved from without by the pressure of public opinion, not like a living thing that moves from within.

VII

PAPAL POWER & INFALLIBILITY

There are quite a number of biblical texts which show that Peter was given by Christ a privileged position among the Apostles. They all confirm the special role assigned to him by Christ and expressed most clearly in the following three texts.

After his profession of faith, "You are the Christ, the Son of the living God," Jesus answered him, "Blessed are you Simon Bar-Jona! For flesh and blood has not revealed this to you, but my Father who is in heaven. And I tell you, you are Peter (Rock), and on this rock I will build my church, and the powers of death shall not prevail against it. I will give you the keys of the kingdom of heaven, and whatever you shall bind on earth shall be bound in heaven, and whatever you shall loose on earth shall be loosed in heaven" (Mt. 16,16-19).

"When they had finished breakfast, Jesus said to Simon Peter, 'Simon, son of John, do you love me more than these?' He said to him 'Yes, Lord; you know that I love you.' He said to him, 'Feed my lambs.' A second time he said to him, 'Simon, son of John, do you love me?' He said to him, 'Yes, Lord; you know that I love you.' He said to him, 'Tend my sheep.' He said to him the third time, 'Simon, son of John, do you love me?' Peter was grieved because he said to him the third time 'Do you love me?' And he said to him, 'Lord, you know everything; you know that I love you.' Jesus said to him, 'Feed my sheep' " (Jn. 20, 15-17).

"Simon, Simon, behold, Satan demanded to have you, that he might sift you like wheat, but I have prayed for you that your faith may not fail; and when you have turned again, strengthen your brethren" (Lk. 22, 31-32) (the you in "have you", "sift you", is plural applying to all Apostles; the others are singular applying only to Simon).

There is no need to cavil about the authenticity of the texts, nor about their application to the person of Peter, nor about the intention of Christ (in the first two texts quoted) to institute a permanent office that was to endure after Peter's death. A community which is to remain united and exercise a number of functions efficiently needs a head. It is the same for the Church as for any state or social organization or business enterprise. Christ evidently chose a government for his Church culminating in one person as the supreme head.

It seems highly doubtful that Christ's words quoted in Luke, 22, 31-32, can also be extended to apply to Peter's successors. They were spoken at the beginning of the passion and allude to a particular trial to which the disciples were submitted, which in Matthew 26,31 is indicated by the words of Christ, "You will all fall away because of me this night; for it is written, 'I will strike the shepherd, and the sheep of the flock will be scattered' ". In both gospels it is followed by the foretelling of Peter's denial of Christ. The disciples failed in their trial and so did Peter, but Peter at once bitterly repented. Therefore, and as their leader, he was best qualified to strengthen the other disciples (in their faith in Christ). The whole episode and its meaning seems to be restricted to this particular situation. There is nothing to suggest that this can be extended to a role Peter's successors also have to fill, or that the giving of strength applies to their ability to guide others in their faith in all revealed truth. A far too heavy load of conclusions is hung on an extremely thin thread.

The Catholic case for papal power is substantially based on the above three texts. In the quotation from the Constitution on the Church, Ch. III, No. 25, we have already noted the teaching authority which is attributed to the popes (page 14). In No. 22 of the same Chapter, Vatican II describes papal power in the following terms: "By virtue of this office, that is, as Vicar of Christ and Pastor of the whole Church, the Roman Pontiff possesses full, supreme and universal power over the Church, a power he is always free to use." As understood, this power does not only apply to the convocation and approval of ecumenical councils, the right to appoint and depose bishops, but extends to even the smallest details, and to every Catholic. Thus he is believed to have the power to regulate the details of liturgical functions and even to impose a foreign liturgical language, to give detailed regulations about the training and life of priests in all countries, and to impose a legislation evolved to meet the needs of a particular country and time – Italy or Western Europe – on the rest of the world. If Eastern Churches are free to chose their own bishops or make their own ecclesiastical laws and liturgical rules, it is by papal concession, not by any strict right. Also the decentralisation of power which has set in with Vatican II is only by way of papal concession, though public opinion will make it nearly impossible to reverse the process. It is still within the pope's power to decide how far it is to go.

The claim to such power (and to infallibility) is an enormous one. It is rejected by all the other Christian churches. Together with the claim of the Church to infallibility, it is the insurmountable obstacle in the way of the reunion of churches. Can it be sustained?

It is based, ultimately, on four figures of speech used by Christ in promising and conferring special powers on Peter. He makes Peter the foundation stone of the Church, gives him the power of the keys, the power to bind and loose, and appoints him as shepherd. Can these figures carry such a load? It is not, of course, a question of how far they can be stretched, what maximum meaning they can be given, but of what Christ did mean when using them.

There are even in the bible some indications that these figures of speech do not necessarily imply such wide powers. In Eph. 2,20, St. Paul calls the Apostles and prophets the foundation on which the Christians are built, Christ himself being the chief cornerstone. In Isaiah, 22,22, the power of the keys is promised to Eliakim, palace steward under king Ezekiah: "I shall place on his shoulder the key of the house of David; he shall open, and none shall shut, and he shall shut, and none shall open"; the office of palace steward comprises only very limited powers. But what is more and perhaps provides the solution to its meaning in the Petrine text, relating well to Peter's profession of faith: Jesus himself uses on another occasion the same metaphor of the key (of the kingdom) to indicate the knowledge required to enter his kingdom: "Woe to you lawyers! for you have taken away the key of knowledge; you did not enter yourselves, and you hindered those who were entering" (Lk. 11,52). The power to bind and loose, expressed in exactly the same terms, is also given to the Apostles generally; in the context it seems to refer to powers of judgement needed to ensure peace in the community: "If your brother sins against you, go and tell him his fault, between you and him alone. If he listens to you, you have gained your brother. But if he does not listen, take one or two others along with you, that every word may be confirmed by the evidence of two or three witnesses. If he refuses to listen to them, tell it to the church; and if he refuses to listen even to the church, let him be to you as a Gentile and a tax collector. Truly, I say to you, whatever you bind on earth shall be bound in heaven and whatever you loose on earth shall be loosed in heaven" (Mt. 18, 15-18). Moreover, these last words of Jesus (of Mt. 18,18) – as others by which he sends them to witness and teach or empowers them to forgive or retain sins – must be applied to the Apostles and their successors also individually. Hence they do not as such signify full power or infallibility. Within the framework of Jesus' own example and of a task regularly expressed in terms of witnessing, teaching, and doing what he has done, they suggest the judicial application of his teaching rather than any power to legislate or to pass judgement on what is true independently from evidence.

It must be admitted, it seems, that the image of the Rock attributes to Peter an essential task in assuring the Church's unity and permanence, and that the other three figures of speech probably imply that he received supreme power. But the objection that must be raised to the Catholic exegesis is that it is vitiated by maximalism. The extent of the supreme power cannot simply be deduced from those figures of speech by giving them a maximum meaning. To gain a total picture of Christ's intentions many other factors have to be considered. To mention some, it must be asked:

1. What is the extent of the demands imposed by the nature of the gospel? Freedom is in possession; its limitations must be proved. No more power has been handed over than is necessary to ensure such unity and direction as the ministry of the gospel requires.
2. What will be most conducive to the spread and effectiveness of the gospel?
3. What are the just claims of the peoples and of the natural values of each cultural and national area?
4. Which church authorities are best qualified to know how the demands of the gospel can be harmonized with and leaven the cultural values, and meet the needs, of each region?
5. Did Christ intend to give to Peter and his successors the power to impose patterns and requisites of one cultural area on another?
6. How did the churches understand papal power in the beginning? The Oriental Churches have largely preserved the original pattern.
7. To what extent can one person, or a few, know and judge and legislate for the legitimate needs of a Church spread out over so many nations and cultures in various stages of development?

To ask such questions is largely to answer them. A community needs a supreme government. But no one would think of asserting that in order to function efficiently a ruler needs absolute power and a prerogative of infallibility. Supreme power operates more efficiently and securely under a system of checks which guards against ignorance and an abuse of power. The fact that the words of Christ, on which papal power rests, do not mention any limits or checks does not mean that no such limits or checks exist. These are known by a study of the nature of things; the essentials of the gospel, the needs of a church spread over so many cultures, the needs of guarding against an abuse of power. To pretend that an abuse of power – *bona* or *mala fide* – is not possible or does not do grave harm to the interests of Christ's gospel and the Christian community is to fly in the face of historical facts. Surely one of the factors responsible for the great eastern and western schisms, and perhaps the decisive one, was the claim to full power made by the papacy and its adherents and the way that power was handled. Used in moderation, within the limits imposed by the demands of the gospel and the diverse needs of each sector of the Church, the supreme power is an important factor for unity; but used without those checks it can easily become a major cause of discord and disruption. The story of Solomon's son Roboam seems to have its parallels in ecclesiastical history.

In our times we have become aware of the disadvantages of an authoritarian and the advantages of a democratic organization of power. There is no reason to believe that a similar development is not desirable in the Church, and entirely in accordance with Christ's will, who does not want the Church to be deprived of the benefits of human progress in the uses of power.* By using only general expressions he

*In a long, thoughtful statement on democratic cooperation in the Church addressed in May 1967 to discussion groups of the diocese of 's-Hertogenbosch, Holland, Bishop J. Bluyssen observed: "Also the layman prophesies, speaks things of God. The consideration that we are God's people contains the task of a genuine democratization. My authority as bishop comes from God, but also yours as member of God's priestly people. If my ability counts, so does yours. If you have to justify your opinions, so have I, to be for you a genuine authority. As you are asked to listen to me, I have to listen to you, to what you as believers and also in doubt or as unbelievers have to tell me" (Katholiek Archief, 1967, No.34, col.855).

left it to the Church and its leaders to develop a system of the use of power which would best meet the needs of the gospel and of each smaller ecclesiastical unit. Such a supposition does not emasculate Christ's words or abolish the system erected by him. There must be one who holds supreme power, and under him, and united with him, other heads in smaller sectors. Within these general lines there is a wide range of possibilities, including that of a very democratic division and sharing of power. In each age and place that form is best which best meets the needs of the gospel, its spread and effectiveness, the legitimate demands of each nation and culture, and the stage of development, primitive or mature, of the Christian people.

It seems evident that while the Church has the task to preach the gospel, all the essentials of it, she has no right to impose non-essentials, patterned to suit the needs of one cultural area, upon another. At the beginning the Apostles did not – after an initial hesitation – impose their own Jewish culture on their converts. When Peter vacillated in his behaviour on this point, Paul "withstood him to the face because he was to be blamed" (Gal. 2). Yet the Jewish customs and forms were those Jesus himself had conformed to. It was therefore an admission that all peoples have a right to their own culture and way of life and that the Church has no right to impose patterns or laws suited to one people or area on another. Later, unfortunately, the temptation arose to identify unessential elements with the gospel itself or give them undue importance. To what lengths this could go, even at an early date, before 200 A.D., we see in the case of Pope Victor who was ready to drive the churches of Asia Minor into schism over such a minor point as the date of Easter. Much worse came later. A whole foreign, European, Latin mould was imposed, together with the gospel, on other areas in Asia, Africa, and the Americas. Where the Church met with primitive cultures she still could meet with a fair success. In the case of the great ancient cultures of Asia this policy raised the most effective barriers possible against the spread of the gospel. The Church paid a heavy price for the eastern schism and for the patronage of the Roman emperors who followed Constantine. It led to an authoritarian and centralized system of government in the western Church, and to a loss of understanding of the true needs of the gospel and of the rights of other peoples and cultures.

In the course of its long history the Propaganda has issued a number of directives to missionaries to respect and adapt themselves to indigenous cultures, but they amount to little compared with the total reality of foreignness with which non-Christians have been confronted. Once created, the wrong image is hard to undo. Changes are easily interpreted as tactical moves, not as an honest admission of an essential distortion of the original image. Moreover, they have continued to be very minor until now. Christianity was very fortunate in entering first the Greek culture with its tradition of logical, scientific thinking. It has, however, helped little in introducing it into the other great cultures, partly perhaps because particular developments in the faith had closed up the channels of fresh thinking before meeting them.

A vast exchange of cultures is taking place which has far from reached its climax. The traditional non-western cultures are taking over the whole of western science and technique and many western ways of living and thinking. To cast the gospel into a cultural mould that is changing rapidly is an extra-ordinarily difficult task that can be accomplished only by those who experience intimately the transition from old to new. All the world's cultures are in flux; they will never again become petrified into patterns that will endure almost unchanged for centuries. Rapid change, optimistically supposed to be for the better, has become modern man's way of life. To keep pace with the vast and rapid cultural changes the Church must herself undertake a continous aggiornamento.* In spite of the growing interchange and

*Many changes are ephemeral and radically affect only minority groups, especially the young; they are no reason for local churches to make general changes (for instance in the liturgy) for all. The best way to meet legitimate demands or needs of minority groups of whatever nature or duration is to allow special provisions to be made for them. Uniformity in non-essentials is convenient for management and mass production; there is less to commend it for purposes of art and religion.

unification of cultures, however, great national and regional differences will remain and the need of autonomy in non-essentials will not diminish. Only the national or regional churches are competent to judge what the gospel in their area needs at a given time. An increasing cooporation of the churches is required, however, to tackle problems that can be solved only by united efforts. This cooperation – as well as the preservation and elaboration of the essentials of the faith – will be guided or supervised by the bishops under the successor of St. Peter.

It is an exaggeration to make it appear as if the role of Peter is the main source of unity among Christians. When Paul spoke of "One Lord, one faith, one baptism" he mentioned other sources of unity. The unity and perdurance of the Church are not only, or primarily, guaranteed by the pope; it is faithfulness to the Lord as he appears before us in the authentic records that alone can guarantee faithfulness also to one human head. Belief in and faithfulness to Christ and the gospel, essential oneness in faith on that basis, can alone provide the pope with sheep to look after. Also, on the level of a visible community, the Church owes its unity and strength infinitely more to a common love of Christ and the gospel than to the one visible head. Unity does not flow automatically from a visible head; it is the reward of a rule conducted in accord with the spirit and needs of the gospel and with regard to the natural rights and needs of the ruled. Christ's commission to Peter did not only grant rights, it also imposed duties. By overstepping its rights or neglecting its duties, the papacy can as easily become the cause of division as it is meant to be a source of unity.

Similar reasonings as have been advanced to prove the infallibility of the Church, are used to prove the infallibility of the pope. It is also argued that since he is the foundation of the Church's unity, he must be able to ensure unity in the faith, which requires infallibility. As shepherd he must be able to provide wholesome pasture, which is truth. Error would be a poisonous food. The reply to these reasonings has already been given when the infallibility of the Church was examined. The ultimate source of certainty is the reliable authentic records, not any claim to infallibility. Only they can guarantee certainty and unity in the faith. Papal definitions only set the seal on generally accepted views; they do not precede, they follow convictions already existing in the Church. No pope would dare to be so irresponsible as to define a doctrine still controversial and not accepted by the Church at large. Not having any special personal knowledge on which to rely, his only source of knowledge is that available to the entire Church.

Theologians commonly accept that there are only two doctrinal* definitions by popes which surely fulfill the conditions for an infallible definition, those on Mary's immaculate conception and assumption with body and soul into heaven. Both defined what was already generally accepted in the Church. It is hard to believe that a definition was really needed or urgent. A prerogative which perhaps has been used only twice in 1900 years, and then only to define doctrines not in urgent need of an infallible definition, seems hardly a necessary prerogative. To this it may be objected that it may be needed more in the future, or that it is always in the background of other papal teaching, giving it more authority. The first is a mere supposition, and it is a fact that the Church managed to resolve its greatest controversies, those of the early centuries, without a firm belief in papal infallibility, through an appeal to the Scriptures. The growing influence of the papacy, its jurisdiction and teaching authority, were unable to avert the great schisms of east and west, apparently were their major contributory cause. Since a papal definition has to follow a conviction already achieved in the Church, it does not seem to be needed to preserve the Church from conflicts; by the time it can be proclaimed, the conflict has already been resolved. The appeal to infallibility does not create a consensus or certainty, it only

*Canonizations of saints, too, are generally considered infallible papal decisions, but their importance is very minor compared with definitions of doctrines.

acknowledges them. General certainty is one of the conditions for its application.

It is said that a religious error of the pope becomes at once an error of the whole flock. With belief in his infallibility this is usually so. There have already been a number of doctrinal positions taken by popes which later had to be revised or abandoned. The fact that the popes had stated them made them generally accepted by the Church and made their revision more difficult. Once it is realized that the pope and the Church are bound to what is clearly contained in Christ's gospel as recorded in the books of the New Testament, any statement can be judged by the Church in the light of the gospel and any mistake committed will do little or no harm. In doctrinal questions Pope and Church will not chiefly be led by existing common opinions, but by what is evidently contained in the bible. The Church as a whole will have a criterion by which to judge its own common opinions and papal pronouncements. As presently understood, infallible papal definitions do not need proof, they are valid even without convincing evidence. They carry the proof of their conformity with truth in themselves. The fact of the definition is sufficient evidence. But is a careful judgement of the Church as a whole, finally brought about by the compelling meaning of the New Testament scriptures, not *a priori,* in ordinary providence, a much better guarantee against error than the judgement of one man?

We have already seen that the biblical evidence advanced for ecclesiastical infallibility is far from compelling. If the evidence for ecclesiastical infallibility is not valid, the case for papal infallibility collapses with it. In asking us to accept the substance of Christ's gospel, God respected our rational nature and provided first-rate testimony, accessible not only to Christ's contemporaries, but also to us. Is it possible to believe that for knowledge of secondary importance he should demand our blind submission to an *a priori* most improbable infallible authority without providing overwhelmingly convincing evidence for its existence?

VIII

INFALLIBILITY & TRADITION

There is no virtue or sense in faithfulness to tradition as such. Tradition passes on good and bad, truth and error, and efficient and wasteful, graceful and ugly, ways of doing things. Tradition cannot spare us the effort of sifting what is true from what is false or of finding more effective tools for today's tasks and needs.

There is probably nothing that has done so much harm to religion, Christian and non-Christian, in recent times as the view that considered all tradition as sacrosanct instead of insisting on the duty to preserve what can be proved to be true and keep a sceptical and open mind on all the rest. By making traditions sacred religion placed them beyond the reach of critical appraisal and correction.

As Christians we are certain that what Christ revealed is true. We base our faith on what reliable historical documents tell us of him. We still face the difficulty of understanding his words and what they imply. A study is needed of the languages and circumstances of those days and of the way Jesus used them to put his message across. Study and meditation on the bible have gone on throughout the centuries. It is most unlikely that any major teaching of his escaped being discovered, also because the Apostles and disciples must have done their best to bring out all the essential facts and teachings quite clearly. But new fine points have been discovered in every age, especially in recent times, in which the knowledge of Palestine at the time of Christ, its languages and customs, and of the laws of interpretation have taken great strides.

What the Church claims is that in addition to the bible she has an apostolic tradition with the help of which she is able to preserve and know revealed doctrines with infallible certainty for which no convincing evidence is available to show that they were really taught by Christ. It is tempting to project later doctrines and practices back into the past and believe that they go back without interruption to the time of the Apostles and Christ. Actually, apart from those clearly contained in the bible, it does not seem possible to prove this for a single practice or belief. When in the latter case we appeal to tradition we do not really appeal to a historically reliable and verifiable tradition, but to tradition as a theological principle; i.e., to a general acceptance at some time or other as sufficient proof, because of a divine guidance, that they are part of the original apostolic deposit. All its value depends on whether such a divine guidance is really given. This cannot be supposed, it is not self-evident, it must be proved.

As noted before, we need not enter into the complex reasonings by which theologians have attempted to explain how propositions which cannot be fully proved, either from the bible records or by an argument from history, as extending back to Christ, can yet be known by the Church with certainty to belong to his revelation. Since the explanations cannot and do not pretend to provide the missing link of evidence, they retain the character of speculations, however ingenious they may be.

Ordinarily the stream of tradition that is passed from generation to generation is composed of true and false beliefs, and only progress in knowledge enables mankind to sift the true from the false. In the process of increasing knowledge new errors creep in that later have to be weeded out. Does the Church escape this law of tradition, at least in religious matters and in things essentially connected with Christ's revelation? Does she escape the law to the extent that she will never definitively hold and teach propositions as part of Christ's revelation which actually do not belong to it?

To say that she passes on the whole of Christ's revelation does not necessarily mean that she passes on only truth, that she cannot also teach errors, or doctrines as belonging to the deposit of faith which she mistakenly accepts as such. There is no contradiction between the two statements: (a) She teaches without fail all the revealed truth and (b) She teaches also a number of human opinions and errors which she mistakes for revealed truth. As long as these errors are not subversive of the revealed truth, leave it intact, they do not deprive us of what spiritual good the revealed truth is meant to convey to us. It is as with food sent to famine-stricken people. The food will feed them and save them from death, even if some of the stuff mixed with it and entering their stomachs is useless or unwholesome. Or it is as with school teachers who, in addition to the truth of the subjects they teach, pass on a number of outdated private opinions.

It is clear from the New Testament that Christ made no attempt to correct all the wrong notions of his listeners and disciples. There must have been scores of them, in addition to the wrong notions due to a literal interpretation of the Old Testament writings. He had an important message to impart and did not wish to weaken or wreck its impact or acceptability by hunting down the many wrong traditional beliefs, also in religious matters, of his audience. In fact Christ could not have succeeded even if he had tried, not at least in any normal course of development, because it would have presupposed in his listeners a knowledge and insight, in many matters, far ahead of their time. Even grave errors which intimately touched on the very essence of his teaching – as the existing opinion on slavery which painfully contrasts with his command of love and with the dignity and rights of children of God – he allowed to persist, leaving to a growing future understanding to correct them. The fact that he did not attack current notions, and even made use of them, was taken as an approval of them. He did not, for example, reject Jewish belief in demoniac possession and by his way of acting gave the impression that he shared the belief, though bible scholars, including Catholics, are now of opinion that the many disturbances referred to as such in the bible were merely psychopathic. He allowed new errors to arise from his own words without, it seems, making an attempt to rectify them. Thus his disciples expected his return and the end of the world within the life-time of their generation and many thought that the Apostle John would not die, an opinion referred to in the last verses of John's gospel.

It is natural to expect that firm religious convictions of the Apostles and their Jewish contemporaries, corrected by Christ in a few essentials only, were handed on to the early Church and considered part of the "apostolic tradition", forming together with Christ's teachings one deposit of religious belief which as a whole was considered guaranteed by the Apostles and Christ himself. This stream must later have expanded with religious notions from non-Jewish cultures.*

To these human traditions was later added a vast flow of theological speculations. When logically following from revealed truth rightly understood, they would be valid. But what if they were based on a mixture of revealed truth and human traditions mistaken for revealed truth, or on revealed truth and opinions accepted for evident which only later knowledge could expose as false? Would not the conclusions enter into the stream of tradition under the guise of revealed truth or of truth necessarily flowing from it?

A few examples will illustrate this. Until recently the Church considered all narrative passages in the bible as

***Many of the notions that are part of the "Christian" heritage are simply specifics of the Jewish and Greek-Roman cultures. Anthropologists have shown, for example, that there is a great variety of sex regulations in different cultures and that on a number of points the existing European or brahminical principles are highly atypical. Is it so sure that we can simply identify the latter with "Christian" ethics and give them an absolute validity for all peoples and conditions?**

substantially historical, including therefore the narrative describing the creation of man and his early fortunes. Hence she taught, as something clearly revealed and to be accepted by all, that God created man, body and soul, by a special act of divine intervention. Only when arguments for evolution became overwhelmingly strong did the Church begin to permit belief in the origin of man's body by a process of evolution. Connected with this is the traditional doctrine of original sin. On final count it was based on the supposed substantial historicity of the paradise story. This historicity can no longer be defended; neither on ordinary historical grounds, since man's origin reaches back over millions of years; nor on exegetical grounds, because it is now clearly understood that the bible is full of contrived stories and legends used to illustrate the authors' religious views. Based on invalid, or at least extremely doubtful, human suppositions, those elements of the doctrine which are due to the supposed historicity of the narrative cannot but share in the weakness of its foundations. We have here a doctrine, and a whole system of doctrines derived from it, which is largely founded on a human tradition which newer evidence has completely shaken. These two instances are particular cases of the implications of the new exegesis, sanctioned by Pope Pius XII and Vatican II, that is itself a surrender of earlier doctrinal positions on how to interpret the bible. This makes it necessary to take a second look at all those traditional doctrines that were based on a literal interpretation of bible texts that seem to demand a non-literal interpretation.

The people of that age attributed to the direct working of God or of supernatural powers what today we know is part of the ordinary working of nature or of the mind of man. * It is clear that Jesus did not try to correct the primitive view

*Related to this pre-scientific state of knowledge is the weakness for turning a simple sequence in time into a causal connection. Even in advanced countries we still meet with many examples of beliefs based on such unscientific reasoning. A grotesque example of it, in a traditional society, is the apparently wide-spread belief in India that the severe droughts of 1965-66 were due to the scattering of Nehru's ashes over the fields and rivers of the country.

of the working of nature. It would have been a hopeless undertaking to do so.

Moreover, though his contemporaries were wrong in attributing many effects to a special intervention of God or of supernatural powers, they were not wrong in ascribing them to God's action: "In him we live and move and have our being." Even if the distinction between God's ordinary and extra-ordinary providence was not quite foreign to them, they were unable to understand that special interventions of God are extremely rare exceptions instead of common daily events. It is obvious that this could easily lead them to believe in a divine inspiration of the bible – a belief shared by other ancient peoples about their religious books – and in a special divine guidance of the Church, on evidence that cannot satisfy people with a much better knowledge of the powers of nature and the human mind.

For the Church the main danger of errors lies in her going beyond the apostolic testimony of the scriptures in reliance on doubtful, human traditions; though another source of errors, of a secondary nature, has been imperfect canons of bible interpretation and primitive views of biblical inspiration and inerrancy. And why should not Christ permit the Church to err whenever she oversteps his authentic gospel? Are not commission and promise given by him limited to it? Though she has come to think that her other beliefs and traditions are also under the guidance of the Spirit, isn't it *a priori* more probable that the Spirit is with her only in preserving and understanding the known authentic gospel and that she is on her own and subject to errors whenever she goes beyond it? There was a time when in our dispute with the evolutionists we thought we knew exactly what nature could and could not do by its own powers. We pointed out the various stages in the process where a special divine intervention had been absolutely necessary. Today we admit that we were mistaken. But we still believe we can exactly say why and where a special divine guidance is required to preserve the Church from falling into error. Has she not made enough mistakes in spite of her claim to infallibility? (See the next chapter.) It does not help to say later that the mistaken doctrines were not taught "infallibly." In practice it does not make a difference for the mass of Catholics, including, as experience shows, priests and bishops, whether or not all the conditions for infallibility are fulfilled; that lies beyond their judgement; they believe whatever the Church teaches for certain at a given time. It was nearly always doctrines not clearly contained in the gospels that later had to be abandoned. It is, therefore, by being faithful to the gospel as proved to have been preserved in the written apostolic testimony, not as presumed to have been preserved by tradition, that the Church is the best guardian and safest guide of faith.

This may suffice to make it clear that the broad stream of ecclesiastical tradition, which in all its major elements was believed to be of divine origin, is actually composed of two streams, a divine and a human tradition, intimately intermixed. It has already been noted, early in this thesis, that theologians have begun to call all traditions ecclesiastical, non-apostolic, which are not either clearly contained in the bible or already infallibly defined. Thus in an article in the August 1967 issue of *Diakonia*, p. 213-4, Bishop J. M. Reuss calls the doctrine of the immorality of all use of contraceptives only an ecclesiastical tradition, not an apostolic one. The same he asserts for the former doctrines on the illicitness of taking interest on loans and of sexual intercourse without the intention of procreation. It is easy enough to state this *post factum,* after a teaching has had to be given up or become doubtful; in fact, however, there are infallible definitions which seem to have no better foundation in the bible than those mentioned. The fact is that apart from the bible the Church has no criterion enabling her to distinguish between so-called ecclesiastical and so-called apostolic traditions. She has been unable to keep them apart; she taught for certain what later proved to be fallible human traditions.

This rules out tradition as a means sufficient in itself to guarantee its truth without other evidence. Loyalty to tradition can only mean that we should not give up traditions without sufficient reasons. It must never come in the way of truth, nor prevent an honest and courageous search for the truth or an acceptance of views with that degree of certainty or probability which the evidence warrants. Truth is the criterion of right or wrong tradition, not tradition the criterion of truth. The Church's passivity and hesitation to face up to new evidence made her appear a citadel of backwardness and reaction.

The task of sifting human from divine traditions can only be done by a twofold advance in knowledge: on the one hand through a better understanding of what the authentic sources prove about the contents of Christ's revelation; on the other through progress in fields of natural knowledge.

The gospel comprises a strictly circumscribed body of events and religious truth. It is Christ's gift to mankind, opening up vistas beyond the curtain of man's visible world, solving his main existential problems. Christ did not in addition take away from his followers all wrong traditional notions, nor give all knowledge required to solve mankind's future religious or moral problems. He gave mankind a shot in the arm potent enough to secure its substantial spiritual health. With this and other God-given means and resources, mankind is equipped to tackle its tasks. The rest is left to good-will, cooperation, study, experience, work. There is nothing to prove that the Church has a monopoly even of religious knowledge. She certainly has no monopoly of knowledge and wisdom to enable her to solve mankind's economic, social, political, and other problems, which are also moral problems of justice, fairness, mutual love. She has much to offer but also much to learn from the non-Catholic and non-Christian parts of mankind. Probably the main contribution Christianity can make to the solution of political, social, and economic problems, is to help raise men, in the name of God and man, above self-serving half-truths to the search for the whole truth which impartially serves the interests of all. Ministers of religion must begin with themselves; they must place truth above their vested interests in God and Church.

IX

INFALLIBILITY & DOCTRINAL CHANGES

The main practical reason advanced for infallibility is that it is needed to give us certainty about what we have to believe. It is clear that, in spite of infallibility, we largely lack such certainty in practice. There have been quite some changes in the ordinary teaching of the Church. Before an analysis is made of the significance of this fact, it will be useful to list a number of those changes.

The best known recent examples of doctrinal change are probably those on evolution and the interpretation of the bible. With his encyclical *Divino Afflante Spiritu* Pope Pius XII officially abandoned the older literal interpretation of the bible and accepted one based on the intention of the authors. With this change whole books, and large parts of others which before had to be accepted as historical and literally true, could be interpreted as illustrative. This still left the obligation to accept as literally true whatever the authors, though according to the manner of their age, intended to be historical. The Second Vatican Council took another step forward by stating that "the books of Scripture must be acknowledged as teaching firmly, faithfully, and without error that truth which God wanted to put into the sacred writings for the sake of our salvation." This clause is not meant as a quantitative restriction. The whole bible is still considered inspired and without error. But it is declared authoritative and inerrant only in what it intends to assert for the sake of man's salvation. This leaves the way open to admit errors even in the historical writings of the bible, which is what many Fathers and theologians of Vatican II intended. The latest changes in exegesis are a culmination of a succession of earlier retreats. When Galileo was condemned, it was on the basis of the doctrine, as then understood, of biblical inspiration and inerrancy. As was already pointed out, the new exegesis demands a second look at doctrines which are based on a literal interpretation of biblical passages which according to the intention of the biblical authors were (probably) not meant to be taken literally.

Another well-known example of doctrinal change is on the morality of lending money at interest. Not only popes but also general councils repeatedly condemned the practice. As late as May 9, 1821, the Holy Office declared that the making of profit from a loan as a loan is unlawful. Canon 1543 says literally: "If a fungible thing is given to another in such a manner that it becomes his own, and is to be later on returned in kind only, no gain may be made by reason of the contract itself. However, in lending a fungible thing, it is not per se illicit to make an agreement about the legal interest, unless it is certain that it is excessive, nor is it illicit to make an agreement for more than the legal interest, if a just and proportionate title justifies such an agreement." To explain the change in doctrine that occurred, appeal is made to a remaining nucleus which is stated to be the unchangeable substance of the doctrine; changes in material circumstances are said to account for the different moral judgement on the situation. Material facts have changed, but not all that much. What is now general was already not uncommon for centuries when the old doctrine still held the field. Loans were accompanied by risks. Merchants made money breed money. There were long periods during which there was an almost continuous devaluation of money. But against all these facts the doctrine, or its application, was maintained as an absolute, divine law. In practice positions are now completely reversed. Taking a moderate interest is generally permitted. What seems to have happened is this. In an agrarian society such as the Jewish, interest on loans was often ruinous to the small farmer. Moreover, the Jews considered each other close blood brothers. They made several laws which favoured the weaker party more than justice seemed to demand. The law against interest must probably be understood against this background. But since it was in the bible and did not evidently bear the mark of a positive law, it was later mistaken for a divine law binding all societies at all times.

Another doctrine which is now understood very differently from before is the one expressed in the misleading words, "Outside the Church there is no salvation."

It is no longer obligatory to believe, with the ecumenical council of Florence, that "souls of those who depart this life in ... original sin alone (i.e. of unbaptized children), go down to hell"...or limbo.

Slavery was generally accepted as a licit institution until quite recent times. So was, at Rome, the castration of choir boys to preserve their soprano voices.

The doctrinal position on freedom of conscience, freedom of public worship for non-Catholics, and the relations between Church and State, solemnly pronounced by Pius IX in his Syllabus of Errors, are very different from those accepted by Vatican II.

Not all today would be willing to accept St. Augustine's view, repeated by Pope Innocent III, that it is sinful to lie even to save an innocent person's life. Those who still hold that to tell lies is always sinful, explain the word lie in a way which in practice allows the same untruths as are admitted by others. It becomes then very much a question of the use of words.

A similar change has taken place in the traditional view on sex which considered its use fully lawful only for the purpose of procreation. Since Pius XI the Church has sanctioned its use even when conception is not possible, and even permits, for good reasons, so to plan its use that only infertile days are chosen.

There is now a rapidly spreading doubt, especially in countries with an independent Catholic press, about many other doctrines such as the morality of the use of contraceptives, original sin, the physical presence of Christ in the Eucharist, the exclusion of women from the sacramental priesthood, the traditional doctrine on indulgences, and others. This seems only a beginning of a break with traditional positions, due to newer learning, after centuries of dogmatic immobilism. As a result, a growing wave of uncertainty and confusion has begun to sweep the Catholic Church, and many have begun to ask the questions: where will it all end? what still to believe? what trust can we still put in the Church's teaching authority? It is too late to stem the tide of doubt with a simple appeal to ecclesiastical and papal infallibility or teaching authority. The pressure of new evidence or new distinctions does not permit simply an appeal to authority. The authority to which appeal is made must rest on evidence for its total claim.

It is argued of course that in these examples of change the infallibility of the Church is not involved since all conditions for its exercise were not fulfilled. As it is mainly a question of the infallibility of the ordinary magisterium which is at stake in the questions mentioned, it may be good to quote again the conditions Vatican II laid down as a criterion for its infallibility. It says, "Although the bishops do not enjoy individually the prerogative of infallibility they nonetheless proclaim Christ's doctrine infallibly whenever, even though dispersed throughout the world, yet remaining in communion among themselves and with the successor of Peter, they authentically teach matters of faith and morals and agree on one position as definitively to be held."

It is interesting to note that this statement omits one major condition mentioned in the famous words of St. Vincent of Lerin who demands that the Church retain as truly Catholic what was believed "always, everywhere and by all". In the statement of Vatican II there is no demand made that the proposition must have been believed "always". In fact there is no mention of time at all as a criterion. The Vatican II criterion applies even when the conditions mentioned are fulfilled only for one or two decades. How important this matter is, is evident from the question of the licitness of the use of contraceptives. There seems no doubt that after *Casti Connubii* of Pope Pius XI, the whole magisterium taught unanimously with the pope that all use of contraceptives is illicit; they taught this authentically, as a matter of morals, and as definitively to be held. This means that according to the conditions of Vatican II this teaching seems to be an infallibly true doctrine of the ordinary magisterium. Yet today a rapidly growing number of leading theologians no longer accepts the proposition as true. If, on the other hand, we accept the conditions as laid down by Vincent of Lerin, and as often quoted in Catholic tradition, we have probably not a single doctrine, except those clearly contained in the bible, for which a convincing proof that it was always generally taught can be established.

In the examples of change of doctrine mentioned above there is no doubt that the earlier view was generally held, for some time, at least in nearly all cases. To show that there is here no question of a change in doctrines infallibly taught, it is said that in the case of the earlier views all conditions for infallibility were not fulfilled, or at least that it has not been proved that they were. If this is admitted, the obvious conclusion is that it is evidently extremely difficult to prove the fulfilment of those conditions. The question then arises: Are there any doctrines taught by the ordinary magisterium, except those clearly contained in the bible, in which the conditions have been proved to be fulfilled? And if they have been proved to be met, is the proof – which is naturally a question of extensive and intricate historical research, accessible only to a few expert scholars – itself infallible? Can infallibility be the prerogative of a small number of research scholars? And if the result of scholarly research cannot be called infallible, as it evidently cannot, how can we say that it is infallibly sure that conditions are all fulfilled? What remains of (the usefulness of) an infallibility, of the ordinary magisterium, of the fulfilment of the conditions of which we can never have infallible certainty? Surely an infallible certainty can never rest on a fallible one, one which is moreover the preserve of a few scholars.

When doctrines have changed, as in the case of the licitness of taking interest on loans or of the meaning of the doctrine that outside the Church there is no salvation, it is argued that the doctrine contains a nucleus which is its real essence that has not changed. The objection to this argument is that the nucleus is only established *post factum,* after all the changes, forced on us, have been written off as non-essential. Before the change took place, it was not known what the unchangeble essence or nucleus in the doctrine was and what was subject to change. When speaking of heresies, it is said that they contain a nucleus of truth. In their case it is not said that because of that nucleus of truth the doctrines are orthodox. In this kind of reasoning one is always right. Words are elastic, and so apparently are doctrines; we can always, in this nucleus theory, stretch them a little more to escape being proved wrong. And why should the infallibility apply only to the so-called nuclei, when in fact the Church's insistence was as much, or more, on the parts abandoned than on what is eventually retained?

After so many changes in doctrines which were thought to have a secure foundation in the ecclesiastical magisterium, this alone can no longer provide a firm basis of certainty. It must appeal again to what Christ taught, as it can be proved from the first-hand apostolic testimony preserved for us in writing in the gospels and other books of the New Testament. An appeal to unsupported authority must make way for an appeal to valid historical evidence. Only on that foundation can we have certainty and regain that unity of Christians of which Jesus promised that it will make the world believe that the Father has sent him.

POSTSCRIPT

By her claim to infallibility the Church ruled out in advance all evidence contrary to her dogmas as invalid and inadmissible. A firm present or past conviction was for her a valid (substitute for) proof. However, the drastic changes and abandonment of some traditional teachings forced on her make conceivable the need of a similar change of attitude towards the doctrine of infallibility. If the evidence is still available on which our ancestors based their judgement, we must be able to re-examine its validity on the basis of the same – and new – evidence. Such re-appraisal on objective grounds requires an open discussion and must be possible within the Church herself. To be able to give a reasonable assent where it is due, each new generation has to re-assess the beliefs of its predecessors. Many old convictions have proved wrong. This makes it no longer possible for us to accept past beliefs as such, without proof. If God makes the enormous demand of belief in the existing doctrine of infallibility, he must have placed at our disposal a correspondingly satisfactory evidence. Texts and facts which, as I have tried to show, can reasonably be explained otherwise, do not suffice for that. Though revolutionary within the Roman Catholic Church, the proposition advanced in this treatise leaves intact the substance of Christianity and Church and the ultimate bases of certainty on which even infallibility must be grounded.

Some people strongly advised me not to publish this thesis. Bishops should keep out of theological controversies and certainly not start them. One wrote, "Even if you are right, you should not publish it; it is better to leave people in invincible ignorance than to make them lose their souls."

It is true that bishops are supposed to stick to their administration; they are supposed to have no time for a serious study of theological problems. The magisterium has become an "administerium". We have come a long way from the early centuries. In those times most theological thinking and writing was done by bishops. Leaving aside Pope Clement, there was not a single pope among the great Fathers of the Church for the first four hundred years. Even today popes are not chosen for their theological competence, and though their election adds greatly to their sense of responsibility, it adds nothing to their knowledge. Should bishops not share responsibility for the confrontation of the gospel with modern problems and thought?*

As for disturbing the peace. There is a growing revolt against the ecclesiastical teaching authority and traditional doctrines. Pope Paul is greatly worried. But the only way out is to face the problem squarely. Moreover, it seems we deceive ourselves if we think that the other Christians will ever accept our positions on infallibility and papal power. Our case appears just not good enough. But on the basis of the gospels we can unite. If we are wrong in our claims, then we are the insurmountable obstacle to Christian unity, and we cannot simply go on in order not to disturb the peace. A true and lasting peace can be established only on the basis of manifest truth, the truth that will make us free.

*A priest suggested to me that dioceses should be no bigger than present deaneries. This would still make them much larger than most dioceses were in the early centuries. It would do away with the grand-seigneur style of bishops, make them intimate companions and co-workers of their priests, and bring them closer to the people. It would also make it possible for those with interest and talent in that direction to study and help tackle today's problems. Since writing this the priest in question, Th. Steltenpool, advocated this idea, with some of its implications for a possible further democratization in the national churches, in the Dutch monthly *Confrontatie*, No.34, March 1968.